Selling Used Books Online

The Complete Guide to Bookselling At Amazon's Marketplace And Other Online Sites

By Stephen Windwalker

Harvard Perspectives in Entrepreneurship
Harvard Perspectives Press

351.4

Published and distributed
By Harvard Perspectives Press
Belmont, Massachusetts
Email: BooksellingBook@aol.com

Stephen Windwalker

Selling Used Books Online: The Complete Guide to
Bookselling At Amazon.com's Marketplace
And Other Online Sites

ISBN 0-9715778-3-8

First Edition, May 2002
First Printing, May 2002
Second Printing, October 2002

Manufactured in the United States of America.

For my family, with amazement and gratitude.

Table of Contents

I   Is This For You?

Is now the time to realize your dream of becoming a bookseller, of working from your home, of using your love of books and your entrepreneurial energy to create a full-time or significant part-time income for yourself and your family?

Running a bookstore is one of those occupations, like opening a restaurant or managing a major league baseball team, which tends to attract a great many individuals with rather romanticized conceptions of what is involved. It's just, you know, what they have **always wanted to do**. To put it another way, at the risk of a bit of literary name-dropping, we can quote the often intriguing 20th century literary critic and memoirist Anatole Broyard:

"To own a bookshop is one of the persistent romances, like living off the land or sailing around the world."

What could be more fun!

Well, get a grip, please. Thousands of people fail at running bookstores, thousands of people fail at running restaurants, and in the process they learn that much of the work involved is not fun at all, much less what they have always wanted to do. Since thousands of people also fail at running fantasy baseball teams, it's probably a blessing that they never get the chance to manage real human beings on major league baseball teams.

Now, the advent of online used bookselling has greatly lowered the stakes involved in failing as a used bookseller. Instead of losing anywhere from $20,000 to $100,000 and having to hire a lawyer to negotiate one's way out of a multi-year lease and a mountain of publisher and distributor debt, a failed online used bookseller might lose $500 and a lot of time and effort. But it remains true that many will fail.

It doesn't have to be this way, so our mission with this book is three-fold:

7

- First, we hope that by providing a candid look at the nitty-gritty of used bookselling, to persuade a significant number of people to do something else for which they may be better suited;

- Second, we believe we can provide and organize information and suggestions that may accelerate progress on the learning curve and make the difference between success and failure for a significant number of current and future online used booksellers; and

- Third, we hope to improve the overall quality and market strength of online used bookselling by helping sellers to raise the bar when it comes to customer service and fulfillment, business practices and efficiencies, diversity of offerings, and pricing strategy, with the result that the ensuing improvement in customer experience will ultimately mean more customers and more selling for the sellers.

Let's start by suggesting some things that would be very helpful qualities if you want both to prosper and to be happy as an online bookseller.

We could make the following into one of those litmus test quizzes where you can score 17 to 20 and be Jeff Bezos or 0 to 3 and be Maynard

Authors, small independent publishers, public libraries, and some charities

Before we go any further, let's make clear that many potential sellers, for whom this book is intended to be useful, will differ from the home-office entrepreneur who is contemplated in this initial chapter. Authors, small independent publishers, public libraries, and some charities all have a ready supply of books and a strong interest in selling them, and if you we urge you to keep mining this book for the nuts and bolts assistance that will help you succeed at creating a direct online sales channel for your books.

G. Krebs, but it would be better if we could make it into more of a conversation. None of these are absolutes, but it would be a good starting point for you to take each of the descriptive lines below, weigh it, and have a conversation with yourself or with a friend or partner about whether it fits you (or the two of you as a team, if you are planning to do this together). If not, is there something that stands adequately in its place? The point is not to determine whether or not you can do it well, "it" being the things one must do as an online bookseller. The real conversation is about whether you will enjoy it enough to continue doing it well, and to grow in your ability to do it, over a year, five years, or ten years. So let's see.

You know and love books. You enjoy being around books and the people who read them. You see books as having terrific powers to entertain, to educate, to illumine, to heal, and to amuse. You love to buy books.

You want to work at home or in a small shop, but you are prepared to treat it like a real job and you can give it an absolute minimum of thirty hours per week. If you can give it 45 hours a week, and you have sources of books to sustain that much work, you will do better, assuming you use your time wisely and don't use up all your time on bookselling message boards talking about what you should be doing.

You need after-tax income of $20,000 to $40,000, and you would love to see it exceed $50,000, but you are not driven by a hunger to become a millionaire. The online bookselling message boards were abuzz on the evening of Sunday, March 3, 2002 with chitchat about the inclusion of a Lyme, New Hampshire woman named Isabelle McMillen in *Parade Magazine*'s annual "What Americans Earn," with a stated income of $45,000 attributed to her chosen profession of "online bookselling." "Is that her gross? Is that her net? How does she do it?" came the recurring questions from dozens of message-posters. The post that got my attention, though, was the one that noted an invitation for her to join the message board but lamented that with 11 pages of eBay listings she was not going to have time to keep up with the myriad discussions on the board. Exactly, I thought. $45,000 can go a long way in rural New Hampshire, and Ms. McMillen and her husband are doing well with www.bookbaker.com because they have a solid business plan, knowledge of the items they buy and sell, and a willingness to keep their focus on their work rather than peripheral matters.

You like, respect, and identify with people and you want to run an honest business. A cheerful disposition and a willingness to deal openly and straightforwardly with the people you encounter in your business will be a tremendous plus, because amongst the hundreds of great people you will encounter, there will also be scattered some real beauts. If you let them get your goat you will lose business as well as less tangible things like peace of mind.

You have some basic business sense, organization, and competence. File folders, spreadsheets, lists, budgets, cash flow planning … are you familiar with these things? Can you learn how to use them if you don't already know how? Does the mere idea of them give you a headache? Remember, nobody is forcing you to take this "job". But if you take it, these things are part of it. Even if you see this as a hobby, you must be prepared to run it like a business.

You don't mind doing some drudgework on a regular basis, but … you are also willing to use your noggin to figure out or borrow ways to "work smart." I've never met a bookseller who didn't enjoy buying books, whether new or used, but after that the unanimity about enjoying specific tasks falls off quickly. Posting books on the net, schlepping books, repairing books, picking and packing books, going to the post office – these are some of the daily rituals. You take pride in doing them well, and you can find ways to do them more efficiently, but it is unlikely you will ever see them either as intellectual challenges or as great fun. If you consider them "beneath you," keep the day job.

You want to choose the books you stock rather than be a slave to the whims of the publishing industry. I am writing this book mostly for the used and antiquarian bookseller, and this one is true for brick-and-mortar used book stores but even more true for online sellers: your focus can be solely on what you want to have in stock. Nobody is likely to "walk in" to your online store and ask why you don't carry the latest literary products of Danielle Steel or Rush Limbaugh, and there won't be any publishers knocking on your door to ask you to take a 96-copy display of Britney Spears' illustrated autobiography.

You enjoy going to yard sales, garage sales, flea markets, libraries, thrift shops, used bookstores, and even the town

dump. If looking for books is drudgery to you, this is not for you. Finding creative ways to build an uncommon inventory may be the single most important element in determining how well you do at this enterprise, so let it be fun!

You get a kick out of the thrill of seeking out, and the joy of occasionally finding, hidden treasures. Maybe this is redundant with the previous point, but in my first writing job as a teen-aged stringer covering the Cape Cod Baseball League I was paid by the column inch, so I have always kind of discounted Hemingway's advice about the need for writers to cut their work relentlessly. It's staying in.

You have available & appropriate space. Appropriate space means space that is clean, dry, well lit, and hopefully not in a fifth-floor walk-up apartment. You need to be able to fill the space with shelving, tables, boxes, and a desk and guard it from the kids, the dog, the cat, and other unforeseen pests. You'll need, at the very least, one good-sized room that offers at least 150 square feet, but more is always better.

You are at least 18 years of age, able to enter into legally binding contracts and obtain necessary licenses, and you have a checking account and a usable credit card.

You are computer literate and you have a good computer with a good Internet connection. More about this later, but being handy with a computer can light your way to a lot of work-saving shortcuts.

You have a reasonably strong back and the ability to lug around boxes of books when you purchase them, when you post them, and again when you sell them.

You have a reasonably strong and comfortable office chair at your computer workstation. Trust me. This may even make a difference in your customer service, and it will definitely make a difference in how your back feels after you post a hundred books online.

You have $500 for startup costs. You may be able to get started on half that much, but as we'll see later $500 will set you up just fine for you first month of business, and from that point on you should be able to meet all expenses easily out of your revenues.

You understand and embrace the central role that marketing plays in any business, and you don't feel the need to take a shower whenever you so much as contemplate things such as using e-mail to build your business, making your prices competitive, or trying to make your virtual bookshop a little more like Amazon's and a little less like the local public library. I can't emphasize this enough. Whenever I listen to online booksellers describe their business, the number of them who refuse to grant any role for marketing in their efforts amazes me. It is truly as if some of them believe that they can post their books online and simply wait for the buyers to start sending money. This is not the world in which we are doing business, and if marketing yourself and your business makes you squeamish or strikes you as a little unseemly, please put this book down and think of doing something else.

As you've read through this, maybe each and every point has been a bulls-eye in describing you. Maybe there have been a few that didn't quite fit, but you could figure out a way around them. So, time to quit the day job, right?

No.

Please.

Stop.

Let me put that another way.

STOP!

Before you make any rash decisions, I strongly urge that you consider your support system. Back in the Eighties, I think the term was "safety net."

If you have a day job, keep it until you have proven to yourself that you no longer need it. That day may come, but there is no point in putting extra pressure on yourself before it arrives. Although I have already suggested that you should have 30 hours a week available to do justice to your future as an online bookseller, I will now contradict myself and declare that it may well be worth going through a transitional period wherein you work at it for 15 to 20 hours a week to get things going. You may well find that you can generate $1,000 a month in income during this transitional period, and if you can do that, then there is a good chance that you can build yourself up to a respectable income if you do it full-time.

But as you build your business, beware of making projections based on too little information. So many online booksellers have had the experience of posting a large number of books online all at once and seeing a significant number of them turn over – or sell -- very quickly, that the phenomenon even has a name. If you post two thousand books this week and they are all competitively priced, you stand a good chance of selling four or five hundred of them in the next 30 days! That tells you a lot about the value of fresh listings. What it does not tell you is what you can expect as a normal inventory turnover rate. So please don't make the mistake of telling yourself that maintaining an inventory of two thousand books will mean ongoing monthly sales of five hundred books.

II   The Bookselling Business: How We Got Here

In the course of announcing his company's first-ever profitable quarter, in January 2002, Amazon founder and CEO Jeff Bezos made a stunning acknowledgement: "Fifteen percent of the orders in the quarter are for used products and that comes from over 100,000 different sellers and we're going to continue to work on that business," said Bezos in an interview with CBS MarketWatch's Susan McGinnis. "Basically any small shop or individual can sell things on Amazon right next to our new products and that's been very successful."

Three months later, Bezos announced that the number of Marketplace sellers had grown by another 50%, and that Marketplace orders in the first quarter of 2002 accounted for 23% of all U.S. orders and 12% of all U.S. units.

The majority of these 150,000 sellers probably do not perceive themselves as merchants, much less as booksellers. It is more appropriate to compare them to the brick-and-mortar used bookstores' phenomenon of the customer who brings in books to sell or trade to the store for dimes to dollars, more or less. For decades these good folk have been the lifeblood of many used bookstores, schlepping in boxes with hidden treasures as well as their fair share of useless junk, graciously accepting short payment for their well-kept, once-read books, and thereby allowing the stores to offer intriguing inventory at inviting prices.

Things have changed. Thousands of these customers now realize that they have a choice. When they finish a book and decide not to keep it on their personal bookshelves, they can offer it for sale online with just a few clicks of the mouse. In all likelihood, it's these reader-sellers and their efforts to stretch their book-buying dollars that comprise most of Bezos' 100,000 sellers. (Apologies here to those sellers who are selling used videos, DVDs, CDs, games, Anna Kournikova photos, and other non-book items on Amazon. Much

14

of what follows in this book may be useful to you, but it is my belief that your numbers would not greatly change the story line here, and it is my intention to leave specific references to your many fine wares out of the text if only to avoid unnecessary cluttering of sentence structure by a writer who already has a tendency to write sentences, like this one, longer than what my Microsoft Word Grammar Checker seems inclined to allow without a struggle).

How Many Online Booksellers Are There?

The question remains, how many of those Amazon "merchants" are actually serious booksellers who perceive themselves as such, whether they are working out of established bookstores, their basements or garages or dens, or local public libraries? It is clear that the number is growing daily, and may well exceed one-third of the overall total: perhaps 50,000 or more self-identified booksellers! Indeed, one of the most venerable booksellers' databases, www.Bookfinder.com, introduces its book-searching function with this brief but remarkable description: "We work with a number of new and used book sellers and listings services, aggregating the holdings of over 40,000 different booksellers on one search engine."

Whoa.

40,000 or 50,000 different online booksellers?

Believe it.

But don't believe it tomorrow, because it will be yesterday's count, and too conservative. We are talking about an ongoing explosion of numbers with a dramatic ongoing effect on our economy, on the book industry, and on the lives of tens of thousands of American families.

By comparison, a recent survey found that the number of "open store" used bookstores in the United States in 1999 was about 4,300, an increase from about 3,800 in 1996. Another 2,800 booksellers were found in the same survey to conduct business by appointment, mail order, or at book fairs. (The survey is part of a report titled ***The***

Quiet Revolution: The Expansion of the Used Book Market, published by Book Hunter Press and available online at www.bookhunterpress.com, which also publishes the regional ***Used Book Lover's Guide*** books).

All of these numbers probably suffer from under-counting, but the number of online booksellers may be the most understated numbers. And if it isn't understated as we go to press with this book in the spring of 2002, it will be in a year. After all, online bookselling scarcely existed in the early 1990s, and it was nothing more than a blip on the radar screen as late as 1996. The number of booksellers and the number of titles available can probably be expected to keep growing at least through the first decade of the 21st century, and perhaps beyond.

Books, after all, are ideal commodities for online selling. They have easily stated identifying qualities such as title, author, and binding, and they are relatively easy to describe as to their condition. They come for the most part in standard sizes and they are especially cheap to ship due to the existence of the United States Postal Service's Media Mail classification, also known as Book Rate or Special Standard Rate.

Books are also the ideal commodities for a home-based, little-money-down, bootstrap business. With a little legwork, they are cheap and easy to acquire, and their compact and standard sizes and spine-out identifying information make them easy to keep in inventory in a relatively small space. And perhaps most importantly, their usefulness does not erode greatly with each reading.

The Changing Role of Booksellers' Bogeyman

All this being said, it is nonetheless a stunning set of developments that has enabled a hundred thousand flowers to bloom, if you will, in the field of online bookselling. Throughout the 1980s and until the late 1990s, it appeared that inevitable economic forces within the bookselling industry were leading to greater and greater consolidation. When I opened a small independent community bookstore in an inner-city Boston neighborhood in 1986 it was correctly seen by some as a quixotic and basically selfless move that was doomed to fail financially because of competition from chain discounters and superstores, mall-sprawl, and the competing bookshelves at the local Super Stop and Shops. In the course of staying open for four years and losing what then seemed like vast sums of money, I had a lot of fun, did some good for the neighborhood, and became very active in the American Booksellers Association, where I found a great deal of sympathy for my somewhat self-interested and sectarian view that chains like Royal Discount Bookstores and Barnes and Nobles stores were out to ruin the world. Independent bookstores were dropping like flies, and it often seemed that they stood a good chance to thrive only in resort towns, college towns, and the toniest of neighborhood shopping districts. The other bogeyman for my bookstore and many of my colleagues' was the specter of skyrocketing rents, and this factor was especially trying for used booksellers who might have the ability to control the cost of inventory but who could be forced to close as rents doubled, tripled, and quadrupled in the real estate boom of the 1980s.

It's funny how things change. By the late 1990s, the chain booksellers had dropped significantly on independent booksellers' lists of the top 10 bogeymen. The new villain on the block was the upstart internet bookseller Amazon, which was out there in cyberspace providing an impossibly diverse inventory with relentless customer service, prices that were often discounted at least enough to offset the customer's cost of shipping and handling, and some groundbreaking efforts to personalize the customer's cyber-shopping experience so as to begin to make up for the absence of the wonderful role a real live bookstore owner or employee can play in suggesting a book that's just right for the customer who has just walked in the door. Founded in Jeff Bezos' garage in 1994 and opened a year later, Amazon grew at warp speed.

Within a short time, while some publishers and booksellers worried that mass-printed books might soon be a thing of the past with the advent of e-books, print-on-demand, and other as yet

17

unimagined manifestations of the information age, Amazon grew to be a significant force in bookselling and was joined online by Barnes & Noble, eBay, Half.com, and several efforts aimed at providing independent booksellers with a collective online marketplace and database for their used books (most notably aLibris and ABE) and new books. Even the American Booksellers Association began to look for ways to assist its members in creating an online presence to compete with Amazon and others in the online selling of new books.

Then Amazon *really* threw the bookselling world a curveball. Beginning very quietly in 1998, Bezos' company began allowing people to share its website and become third-party sellers there by posting books for sale and linking them directly to Amazon's listings. Although there were certainly glitches along the way, Amazon generally made it easy for sellers and buyers to connect, complete simple transactions, and quickly move both books and the funds paid for them (less a percentage for Amazon, of course) to their intended destinations. Initially Amazon's percentage, even with credit card fees included, amounted to an average total of only 7 to 10 percent, and as participation in this "zShop" program gradually increased the natural question began to arise: why would Amazon cannibalize its own revenues by inviting competitors, however tiny they might be, to waltz right onto the Amazon website, undercut Amazon's prices, and take away sales that Amazon would otherwise surely make? There were myriad speculations as to the answer, and certainly there was no small amount of understandable fear among zShop sellers and other new and used independent booksellers that Amazon had set in motion a truly sinister monopolistic strategy aimed at bringing its competitors under its big tent only to make them so dependent on Amazon's customer base and brokering role that they would be the proverbial bugs on the windshield when, ultimately, Amazon pulled the plug on its third-party seller programs.

Amazon's Business Model

In November 1999 other possible answers began to become clear. Responding in part to the very specific and direct competition embodied in eBay's newly acquired and fast-growing fixed-price Half.com venture, Amazon began to expand and standardize its third-party seller programs dramatically through the development of a Marketplace program that allows sellers to link books (as well as movie, music, and other products) with extremely high "above-the-fold", first-screen visibility right next to Amazon's own listings. The number of Marketplace sellers began to grow very quickly and within a few months there were numerous individual titles where "glut" conditions forced prices down to ridiculously low levels, a problem that was also in evidence at Half.com.

But for every mass-market John Grisham novel selling for a penny there were plenty of other used books selling for $5, $10, $20, $40, and more. And Amazon, by increasing its per-transaction percentage to 15 percent, raising its monthly Marketplace "Pro Merchant" participation fee to $39.99, and quietly slicing off for itself a significant percentage of the amount charged customers for "shipping and handling", was suddenly operating with a gross margin in the 25 to 30 percent range on its Marketplace transactions – the same profit range it achieves on its own in-house book sales!

While it is true that Amazon must be realizing a much lower dollars-per-transaction yield on these third-party used book sales than on new books from its own warehouses, this is where a better understanding of the true Amazon business model comes in handy. The company that Bezos started in his garage in 1994 has consistently placed its primary faith in the notion that its ability to create positive customer experiences is what drives its business. From a customer experience point of view, the Amazon Marketplace venture means lower prices, a huge increase in available inventory both of newer products and out-of-print titles, the opportunity to search for something hard to find without leaving Amazon's friendly confines, and a chance to significantly reduce the ultimate net cost of purchasing any item by turning around and reselling it when one is finished with it. All of this means more customers and more repeat customers, and Amazon may just be the most successful merchant on- or off-line, since the decline of the Sears, Roebuck catalogue, at winning repeat customer business. Because of the relatively high fixed costs of maintaining its remarkable multi-channel infrastructure, every profitable transaction Amazon can wring out of its Marketplace business improves the company's profitability, its long-term chance for success, and the base of customers who might buy bigger-ticket items down the road while relieving its need to pay the considerable costs of purchasing, warehousing and fulfilling its own in-house inventory.

Amazon's commitment to the "customer-experience" model as the driving principle in its business model and the litmus test for strategic decision-making was proven once again early in 2002 when it opened the door wide to its competitors' *new* book products. Until late in 2001, any seller wanting to post a new book on Amazon's Marketplace had to list it as a used book in "Like new" condition and price it at least 20 percent below Amazon's often already discounted price, which of course meant a razor-thin or possibly negative gross margin after also accounting for Amazon's 15% transaction fee. Late in 2001 Amazon cracked the door open slightly for new products, allowing sellers to opt for a "New" listing with a price-point only 10% below Amazon's price, but with the rather limiting restriction of being visible to Amazon customers only when Amazon's inventory on a particular title went out-of-stock. Not too inviting.

Then, suddenly and without fanfare, in January 2002 the door was opened wide. A seller can now list an item as new and it will be listed right next to Amazon's copies for the customer's choice, and the only price restriction is that it cannot be priced *higher* than Amazon's listed price. This freedom to compete with Amazon for new book sales on its own site is sure to appeal to the full universe of booksellers including used booksellers with as-new items, new-book sellers who have heretofore steered clear of Amazon, wholesalers and jobbers such as Baker & Taylor, Koen Book Distributors, and Ingram, and large and small publishers alike. Interestingly enough, the result is that we are now very close to coming full circle from the point at which Amazon was seen by many independent "new book" booksellers as the bogeyman to a new day wherein Amazon could well play the role of savior for many independent stores that have the challenging combination of great selection and weak traffic or poor location.

Once again, the charge will go forth from Amazon's detractors, stock shorters, and others who are slow to understand the company's business model, that the company is cannibalizing its own revenues. But is that what's happening here? Not for a moment. Amazon will continue to make a nice 25 to 30 percent slice from all the transactions of all the aforementioned potential Marketplace sellers, without having to warehouse a single book. To be sure, many of Amazon's customers will want to buy only from Amazon's in-house inventory out of fear that the Marketplace experience will feature substandard fulfillment or customer service, credit card security, or email or identity security. But Amazon has committed itself to this model and has already been quite successful in making these transactions seamless and user-friendly for both sides, and one can be sure that it will continue to pay close attention to these issues.

A Marketplace in the Classic Sense

Indeed, the "Marketplace" name says it all. Amazon's goal is to create a multi-channel, multi-product marketplace, almost in the classic sense of the Greek *agora*, that will meet virtually all of its millions of customers' online shopping needs, and to allow market forces to dictate as much of the customer experience as possible, even if it means driving prices on some mass market paperbacks down to a penny a pound.

One result of all of this, of course, is that Amazon continues to capture a greater and greater share of the growing number of internet-connected consumers in the world, and that more than any other group of visitors to any other website, Amazon's customers come to the site with their credit cards handy (or already on file), ready and usually eager to buy books and/or other products.

One increasingly clear result for booksellers is that practically everyone is selling on Amazon, including a growing number of independent booksellers who are stalwart members of the American

Booksellers Association, and even some former online competitors such as aLibris.com. If you want to sell books online, ignoring Amazon or refusing to sell there because you feel it is the independent booksellers' bogeyman is like wanting to open a brick-and-mortar bookstore and ignoring the old maxim that the three most important factors in determining a retailer's success are "Location, location, and location." You can turn your back on Amazon's customer base, but why would you want to do that? Ideology? Please.

(Don't get me wrong; I am an ideologue, but I fail to see a real ideology here).

While Amazon controls a huge share of the online book market, it is not alone by any means. The eBay auction site, which bills itself as the world's largest marketplace, continues to thrive, turn a tidy and consistent profit, and provides the channel for plenty of book transactions. Indeed, when a Lyme, New Hampshire woman achieved instant notoriety in March 2002 by appearing in *Parade* magazine's annual feature on "What Americans Earn" with the listing "Isabelle McMillen, Online bookselling, $45,000, " a little sleuth work by her colleagues on the Bookfinder Insider online message board turned up the news that she sells almost exclusively on eBay. She and her husband sell rare and antiquarian books and ephemera through their www.Bookbaker.com site, with occasional listings at Christie's in New York, and they are obviously finding plenty of eBay customers for items that they couldn't possibly list on Amazon and have chosen not to list at sites such as aLibris.com and Advanced Book Exchange.

A Backlash by Authors and Publishers

One of the more predictable responses to the increasing, and increasingly inexpensive, availability of used books on the Internet has been the opposition of publishers and some authors. The Authors Guild, a trade group for writers, sought to bring this issue to a head in April 2002 with an email calling on its members to boycott

Amazon by ceasing to link to Amazon from their own Web sites, citing Amazon's "notorious used-book service."

"Amazon's practice does damage to the publishing industry, decreasing royalty payments to authors and profits to publishers," the guild wrote in its message. "There's no good reason for authors to be complicit in undermining their own sales."

On April 10, 2002, a copyrighted **New York Times** article by reporter David D. Kirkpatrick said that in December 2000 "the top executives of the Authors Guild and the Association of American Publishers protested in a conference call with Jeffrey P. Bezos, chief executive of Amazon. The executives were particularly upset that Amazon was offering used books for sale at the same time as the books' original publication.

"That suggested that free copies sent to potential reviewers were turning up for sale as used books at Amazon.com, usually for a small fraction of the retail price. (Selling review copies as used books was previously limited to stores in New York and other media centers)," wrote Kirkpatrick, without revealing how he'd reached this remarkable conclusion.

"The Authors Guild asked its members to 'delink' from Amazon.com yesterday because of its latest innovation for selling used books among consumers. Amazon added a new Web page reminding returning shoppers what their previous purchases were and advising them how much they might earn by reselling them through Amazon," wrote Kirkpatrick in the **Times**. Kirkpatrick shied away from the logical questions of how many Author's Guild members have websites or what kind of economic power might be invested in these sites.

"The memo from the Authors Guild suggested that its members link their Web sites with Booksense.com, which is operated by a network of independent bookstores, or BarnesandNoble.com, which sells used books only from a separate part of its Web site," wrote Kirkpatrick in the **Times**.

"Marie Toulantis, chief executive of BarnesandNoble.com, said it had decided that linking its sales of used and out-of-print books to new books 'would cannibalize new-book sales and be a disservice to authors and publishers'," wrote Kirkpatrick in the *Times*.

"Total online book sales account for less than 10 percent of all book sales, according to the Ipsos-NPD Group, a market research company, so online sales of used books are not soon likely to bankrupt the industry. But even a few percentage points of lost sales are important to a slow-growing industry like book publishing," wrote Kirkpatrick in the *Times*.

"Still, Thomas H. Cook, an author who won an Edgar, the award for mystery writing, said that for individual authors the dispute was about principle and the long-term future of the industry. And there were emotional wounds as well, he said.

"'I checked on *The Chatham School Affair* — my book that won the Edgar — I think used copies were going for 25 cents,' he said, 'It doesn't feel great. Part of it is sheer vanity, that you think your book would be worth more than that under any circumstances,'" wrote Kirkpatrick in the *Times*.

Food for thought, but I suspect most booksellers and many authors understand that this "protest" is silly, wrongheaded, and ineffectual.

One point that the protesters seem to miss is that *many members of the book buying public are increasingly willing to lay out folding money for new books*, whether on Amazon or at the local brick-and-mortar shop, if they believe that they can recoup a significant portion of their original price by reselling the book. That's been true as long as there have been used shops willing to take books for cash or trade, but it is obviously truer than ever now with the easy reselling available on Amazon and Half.com.

At least at this writing, it is also still true that the vast majority of books sold on Amazon's site are being sold by Amazon at Amazon's prices, even when there are much cheaper copies available on the same screen. Yes, we subversives here are trying to drive that percentage down, but as of the first quarter of 2002, it was still 77%.

By the way, having failed to grow up in a small Cape Cod town, I read Thomas Cook's *The Chatham School Affair* with great pleasure. It's a well-written book with complex, almost literary structure. But it's just plain goofy to *complain* that a mass market version of the breakthrough mystery novel Cook published six years ago is selling for a quarter in a secondary market. He's already made very good money on it. Next he will be complaining that there are public libraries allowing borrowers to read it for free!

And the real point that he is missing if he has any confidence in his writing, which he should, is that for every reader who happens to pick up *The Chatham School Affair* at any price and enjoy it, there is one more likely buyer for Cook's newest book, *The Interrogation*, on the streets two weeks ago at this writing and weighing in at 1,188 on Amazon's best-seller list. It's called free marketing, Tom!

As for the BarnesandNoble.com claim that linking used books to new books on its site "would cannibalize new-book sales and be a disservice to authors and publishers," one has to wonder what priority BarnesandNoble.com gives to its own customers' experience in its calculus of competing claims, which may help to explain why BarnesandNoble.com is losing market share to Amazon.

While it has always been possible for readers and reviewers to resell their once-read books or unread review copies to used bookstores for dimes to dollars and thus add to their budgets for buying more new books (or groceries), Amazon resellers ordinarily get far more return for their books than sellers at brick-and-mortar shops or at Half.com, so the Amazon argument that its used-book sales actually strengthen its new-book sales is an especially strong one, and is further strengthened by the ease with which an Amazon customer can simply click on an author's name to pursue an interest in that writer's work. As *A Beautiful Mind* author (and Authors Guild board member) Sylvia Nasar wrote in an April 17, 2002 *New York Times* opinion piece challenging the Authors Guild position, the situation is reminiscent of the one in which "car companies often brag about the resale value of their models."

It's occasionally tough for Marketplace sellers to see how our interests are served by Amazon's "customer-experience" centered business model. Sometimes our short-term interests suffer. But it is just a chapter in a longer story. I'm sure I am not the only who recalls that Marketplace was an inevitable institutional response to the development and growth of Half.com. Amazon's move to position itself in that market was good business sense, and while hopefully one can identify self-serving motives in any good business decision, it was also motivated by the need to make sure the customer experience at Amazon was as good as that offered by its competitors. Before there was a "Marketplace", zShop listings were **very** prominent, but there were not many sellers because it was so new. What's changed, as it inevitably would have regardless of the platform used, is the flow of sellers into these venues in the used book business.

What Does the Future Hold?

The next phase in the annals of online bookselling is likely to include interesting regroupings, new databases, partnerships, consolidations, and collapses, and while it is impossible to predict exactly what shape these will take, it is nonetheless clear that for the most part they will be peripheral to the main action in the center of the ring, where Amazon, Half.com, and Half.com's parent eBay strengthen their already strong roles and position themselves relative to each other, their millions of customers, and their tens of thousands of third-party sellers.

As these events unfold, it seems safe to make a few predictions about the effects that they will have on the third-party sellers for whom this book is intended:

Price competition. Online used booksellers will face constant price pressures, not from buyers but from their own ranks, with the natural and predictable result that the sellers who thrive will be those who operate their businesses most efficiently, anticipate and avoid online inventory gluts, and are able to constantly upgrade, diversify, and freshen their inventory while staying one step ahead of the price competition. The online bookselling markets have already reached the saturation point for over-exposed mass market paperback bestsellers, but – please pardon the tautology here -- that saturation point is a long way off for harder to find books.

"Corporate" third-party sellers. A growing portion of the "third-party" online booksellers on Amazon.com will consist of corporate entities including publishers, distributors, and bookstores, although some of the distributors who are currently buying publisher offerings at 55% off, with 90 to 120 day fully-returnable terms, may find that they are jeopardizing their wholesaler discount agreements with publishers by competing with retail sellers under misleading "handles" on Amazon.com's Marketplace.

Bookseller or Broker? Amazon itself may well reach a point where half or more of its book transactions involve third-party sellers. If this happens it will be driven by two major forces: the continued strength and growth of the used book Marketplace initiatives and the decision by a critical mass of authors, publishers, and distributors to take the plunge into the direct retail channel offered by the Marketplace.

A "Universal" Catalog on Amazon's Marketplace? Now that Amazon has revolutionized the world of selling new and recent used books online and has welcomed its competition under its big tent to participate in these enterprises, what would be the next logical expansion of its bookselling tent? Amazon could put out the welcome mat for all of the used and antiquarian booksellers who currently focus their efforts elsewhere by expanding its in-house and Marketplace book catalog to include or allow inclusion of … well, there's not really a modest way to put this, so here goes … *every book ever printed.* The market implications of such an expansion are probably every bit as monumental as the programming and infrastructure challenges that would be involved in achieving it.

Lowballing. The relative handful of online used booksellers who participate in online bookselling message boards will continue to charge each other with price lowballing, but these charges will continue to have

Challenging the Lowballing Premise

If you start feeling that the only way you can sell your books online is to price them at hideously low prices, try testing the assumption. What we do here at Windwalker Books is simply to record some basic information in a spreadsheet for each sale, to see what the data says about price competition vs. other selling points. So far the most interesting conclusions are:
- roughly 50% of our sales occur in cases where our item does not have the lowest price;
- condition is more important to buyers than price;
- less than 5% of our sales occur on titles that are in Amazon's top 10,000 in Sales Ranking; and
- over half of our sales occur on items where the Amazon Sales Ranking is over 1,000,000; and
- about two-thirds of our sales occur on items where Amazon does not have the item in stock.

None of this is shocking, but it is nice to see confirmation of my gut feeling that *finding uncommon books in very good condition and pricing them fairly is the formula for success in online bookselling*. Easier said, of course, than done.

no effect as the sellers who do best will be those who offer the best products and best service at fair prices.

Equilibrium. The increasingly universal availability of good used books at good prices will begin to create price pressures and reduced title availability for the book publishing industry, which may in turn intensify the demand for used books and help create greater supply and demand equilibrium in the used book market on Amazon, Half.com, and elsewhere.

Tightening Supply. The supply of used books available to would-be sellers will gradually tighten both because of the increased demand just noted and also because more of the usual sources will themselves become sellers, and this in turn will feed market equilibrium.

A Change in Publisher Behavior? The books that will suffer most, as a result of Amazon's Marketplace and Half.com, are the hyper-common books that are mega-published by publishers. The major publishers have not had to serve the reading or writing public very well to make their profits in recent years: they just find a hoss like Grisham, Clancy, or King, ride it hard, and put it away wet. In time, it may well be that the market forces unleashed by Amazon and Half.com will force publishers to ratchet down those seven-figure print runs and bring a wider and more diverse array of titles into print and actually market them to the reading public. That would be good for writers, booksellers, and readers in the long run, and I am also convinced that Tom Clancy will survive. Unlikely as it is, one can even imagine a publisher's decision to regulate the flow of copies of a new title so as to support its price in secondary markets.

Whither the E-Book Revolution? The increasingly universal availability of good used books at good prices will tend to slow the growth of e-books and related concepts such as print-on-demand and diminish the likelihood of concomitant predictions of the demise of the mass-printed book.

Library and Charity Competition? An increasing number of public libraries and charitable organizations will establish their own online sales channels at Amazon, Half.com, eBay and elsewhere in order to take advantage of their free, donated sources of inventory and their volunteers' capacity to provide free data entry and fulfillment services. The problem with this, of course, is that these libraries and charities are currently, quite often, the best and cheapest sources of books for used booksellers. If this trend were to advance too quickly, it could have a serious negative effect on used bookseller inventories and actually force some of the more isolated or less resourceful sellers out of business. We are a long way from that at this writing, but American used booksellers would be wise to be alert to the possibilities suggested by this March 2002 report from London's *Daily Telegraph* newspaper on used bookselling across the pond: "Oxfam is now the largest second-hand book dealer in the UK, selling 6 million books a year, mainly at 40 specialist bookshops. It has even set up an online auction site (www.oxfam.org.uk/shop) and deals on abe.com...."

Prosperity and Happiness. Thousands of independent third-party booksellers will make a decent living selling used and antiquarian books, and a few will make a very, very good living. With any luck, a growing percentage will enjoy their work and the special freedoms and pleasures it offers.

These predictions themselves, let me be clear, are worthless, except inasmuch as they provoke booksellers to think for themselves about our enterprise, its future, and how we fit into it. It's worthwhile before going forward for us all to take a step back and realize that the economic forces at play here will always mean that many will succeed at online bookselling and some will fail, because the transparency of the internet combined with the sheer number of sellers, buyers, and transactions allow classic market forces to operate in an extremely pure and uninhibited fashion.

By now it is probably clear that I think it is important for online used booksellers to keep up with, and think intelligently about, what is going on our business. There are a lot of ways to stay up to date, but some of them such as spending several hours a day reading and participating in seller message boards are very time-consuming, and some of them such as subscribing to *Publishers' Weekly* are very expensive (although it is available to read in most public libraries). Here are two cheap and efficient suggestions. First, register online for a free online New York Times subscription and navigate your way to signing up for a daily e-mail alert for articles on the "book trade." This will net you a handful of e-mails each week giving you a heads up about articles that are often germane to your business from a publication that does a pretty good, if occasionally slanted, job of keeping up with the book industry. Second, register as a visitor to *AuctionBytes* at www.auctionbytes.com and sign up for its email newsletter as well. Although it is obviously more associated with online auctioneering than with fixed-price or storefront enterprises, *AuctionBytes* does an excellent job of keeping up with what is important for online sellers.

For a long time many booksellers, including myself, have been concerned about the big eating the small, to use the unpleasant imagery of today's business bestsellers. We got it wrong. Amazingly enough the big are enabling the small to make a good living, and the real and necessary cannibalism of this phase and the next will more likely involve the fast eating the slow. Price competition will certainly force some large and small online booksellers out of business, or into settling for a hobby where they had hoped for a thriving business. But the natural equilibrium of the market will mean that more sellers will figure out ways to adapt and to find and offer desirable titles and price points.

It's Really Quite Simple

The world of online selling provides two huge advantages to its participants. First, it liberates us from paying expensive commercial rent, which I believe is in fact the biggest bogeyman that has been faced by brick-and-mortar booksellers during the past twenty years, perhaps longer. Second, it makes physical location irrelevant (from a selling point of view) while offering sellers direct access to tens of millions of customers.

Turning these advantages into the basis for a profitable enterprise, then, is just a matter of figuring out how to organize an efficient business wherein you can get desirable books as cheaply as possible, offer them to the largest possible customer base at prices that find a workable balance between the buyer's hunger for a bargain and your hunger for a profit, and ship them safely and swiftly with a friendly and professional approach that builds good will.

It's really quite simple, if you take it step by step and keep using your noggin to anticipate the market. So let's begin.

III   Beginnings: Establishing An Identity For Your Online Bookshop

Where should you begin, if you want to start selling books online and you haven't done it before? Well, here's an idea. I recommend that you read this book from cover to cover before taking a single other concrete step toward establishing an online bookshop. You may reject every idea you find here, but I am confident that you'll know even better why you are going to do things the way you are going to do them, if you first subject yourself to the ideas and suggestions contained herein.

Determining Your Business Identity

Every business has a "brand" and culture that is identifiable to its customers, even if the owner of the business is utterly oblivious to this fact. For most sellers operating within the Amazon Marketplace, a big part of that "brand" is provided by Amazon and is not immediately in our control, but there are other elements that we do control or influence including our shop name and its connotations, the kinds of communication and information we provide individually to buyers, the presentation of our business and its policies on Amazon, the contents and average rating in our customer feedback file, our selection, prices, and areas of specialty, the condition of books we ship, the promptness with which ship, the care we use in packaging, and the way we handle complaints, confusion, and requests for returns or refunds. As important as each of these things is individually, it is equally important that they all fit together into a coherent "identity" or "culture" for a business.

Many sellers devote a good deal of time to processes such as deciding upon a store's name or writing the text that will appear on its storefront, and I agree with the premise upon which this investment is made: what a prospective buyer sees, when surfing around Amazon and often making impulse buying decisions, is very important.

When I opened a brick and mortar store called the Dorchester Reading Authority in Boston in 1986 I tried to achieve a tone and culture reminiscent of the Prairie Home Companion radio show that was peaking in popularity at that time; mine was the first and only bookstore in a very urban community of over 100,000 people, and the "motto" on our bookmarks, stationery, and newsletter made the modest claim that "You won't find a better bookstore around here."

Years later, in establishing my first Amazon storefront, I figured that the main constant that any prospective buyer would be looking at when determining whether to buy a book I had listed, as opposed to some other similar copy from a competitor, would be the name I gave my storefront. (They would also see price and description, but those of course would not be constant on all items). I wanted to hit on a name that somehow communicated a brand identity. Noticing that I was listing books for half their retail price triggered fond memories of Sunday afternoons spent browsing a terrific used bookstore during my community organizing days in Dallas in the 1970s, and I decided to call my storefront Half-Priced Books, never imagining that the used bookstore Ken Gjemre had operated in a converted laundromat in Dallas in those days would still be in operation, let alone be the flagship of a chain of dozens of stores in at least eight states. Fortuitously, I suppose, I had forgotten that Ken had decided to call his store Half-Price Books (www.halfpricebooks.com), without a "d", when he opened his first store in 1972. In any case, after I had been selling online for a year or so I started to become aware that Half-Price Books was still in business, and that, not surprisingly, it was also selling books online. I resolved that, if ever contacted by their attorneys, I would point out the existence of the "d" in my business name and let them know that it was not accidental, communicating, at least to any teacher of good grammar, if there are such beings around any more, that Half-Price Books was selling books that were **worth** only half the list price, while Half-Priced Books was selling books that had been **priced** by us at half the list price. Pardon the digression. Ultimately, as market pressures drove prices down at Amazon's Marketplace, I decided that Half-Priced Books was no longer a good brand identity, and changed our name to give respect to my Cherokee handle by making it Windwalker Books, which obviously does not communicate any single brand message to most prospective buyers, but I like it.

As important as it is to establish a brand identity, it is equally important, I think, to establish an "internal" culture for your business, and I would suggest that establishing that culture, for an online bookseller, involves determining the answers to the following questions and then, of course, making them operational:

• What are your goals? Are you trying to supplement a paycheck or social security, eke out a living for one, support a family, or make the Inc. 500 or Fortune 500 list? How much time will you devote to your business? (And that means working time spent acquiring, listing, shelving, picking, and packing books, not time spent reading bookseller message boards! Reading this book, however, counts as work time.) I believe a seller must set sales goals a month, a quarter, and a year into the future and must review performance against these goals with a cold analytic eye at the end of each period to determine what must be changed in his business plan.

• What is your ideal inventory level? How many desirable, appropriately priced new listings do you intend to list each day, each week, or each month? The answer to this last question is the single most important indicator in determining how successful you will be. *Too many times I have seen booksellers complain about declining sales in remarks like this: "I set up shop six months ago with 1500 titles and sold over 500 of them the first month, but now even though I still have 700 titles listed I am only selling two or three books a day." My answer is simple: "if you aren't listing, you aren't selling!"* And the corollary of course is that you must constantly be refreshing the titles that have remained unsold the longest. I believe a seller must set daily or weekly goals for how many new titles will be added to his online inventory and how many previously listed titles will be refreshed. Refreshing previously listed titles, by the way, is not simply about lowballing. Sometimes it means re-linking a title, reviewing and occasionally

34

changing its condition classification and/or description, and possibly increasing its price in a different classification. Sometimes it means deciding that it is time to donate a book to the local public library, so that one of your competitors can buy it from the library and try his hand at selling it online.

• What standards will you set for your business with respect to the quality and condition of books you will acquire for resale, promptness of your shipments, care and quality in packaging, and communications with buyers including sending prompt confirmation messages?

• How much space will you devote to your business and how will you organize and protect that space to ensure that books remain in the same condition and you can pick them efficiently for packing?

The decisions, of course, do not end there. What kind of online bookstore do you want to operate? Should you specialize? Are you going to focus on rare and antiquarian books, a general stock of contemporary used books, or some of both? One needs to establish working answers to these questions to get started, even if you believe that the answers may change over time as you gain experience and build your business.

• Unless you already have significant experience with collectible books, I strongly recommend that you begin by building your business as a "general stock" bookseller and deal primarily with more or less contemporary used books. These books are easy to acquire without much risk to your capital, they will be easy to list for sale, and if they are titles that have not already flooded the market and they are in desirable condition, they will be relatively easy to sell to the non-collecting customers who make up the vast majority of online book buyers. Then, if you are interested in venturing into the collectible book business, you will be able to build your knowledge as you occasionally come across collectible volumes and conduct the research appropriate to acquire, describe, price, sell, and ship them. You can make a good living at either end of this spectrum between selling collectibles and selling contemporary used books, or as a hybrid somewhere in the middle.

Are You a Joiner?

If so, there are numerous organizations that would love to have you and your membership dues, and perhaps even your participation.

The **American Booksellers Association** (www.bookweb.org, email: info@bookweb.org) used to be a fine organization (when I was a member in the '80s) but currently is burdened by the unfortunate combination of very high membership dues ($375 a year) and a dinosaur mentality when it comes to the world of online bookselling.

The more moderately priced **Independent Online Booksellers Association** (www.ioba.org) just lowered the annual dues for its 196 members from $95 to $60, and seems in my judgment to be at a crossroads at which it must determine whether it will actively court the people, for instance, for whom this book is intended or perhaps take a stodgier, more "antiquarian-oriented" and perhaps more snobbish perspective. In the meantime, the weekly "IOBA Monday Item" email from the proprietor of member **J Godsey Booksellers** may well be worth price of membership. In addition, there are regional bookseller associations in every part of the country as well as a number of antiquarian bookseller groups.

Where you ultimately situate yourself will probably depend upon what and who you enjoy dealing with, your ability to educate yourself on the finer points of either market, and your access to good sources of the books you want to sell. Nurture your capacity to develop a "feel" for the books with which you are dealing, and select a few areas where you are knowledgeable to develop expertise and specialization.

Establishing a Culture

While it is important to determine the **content** of your store, it is equally important to establish its **culture**. I will not spend much time in these pages preaching to you about how you should behave as an online bookseller, but I have sufficient reverence for the profession that I feel compelled to state the following.

You are part of, or you are entering, a noble profession, an honorable, ages-old enterprise. Against our increasingly troublesome social backdrop of noise and rudeness, the independent bookseller has long stood for civility, for community, and of course for creativity and imagination. This tradition has been burnished by generations of the best independent booksellers, and we should expect no less of ourselves as online booksellers.

What does that translate into, either on a day-to-day operational basis or in establishing the branding and policies that you will present as your business identity to the online book-buying public?

First, let civility and helpfulness infuse every interaction with your customers, with other sellers, and with vendors from the staff at your local library sale to your contacts at Amazon (they will never admit it at Amazon, but they *are* our vendors, or at the very least our cyber-landlords). The tone of these interactions will of course come back to you, and your days (*and* your nights) will be more pleasant if what comes back is civil and helpful. To be sure, there will be customers who try your patience or tax your credulity, who try to get something for nothing, who expect you to pay for their errors, or, worst of all, who treat you rudely or disrespectfully. In some cases they have other issues and need a kind of help that you are neither equipped nor paid to provide for them. Regardless of that, you will be rewarded with greater peace of mind if you deal with them in a friendly, helpful, and professional manner and move on as quickly as possible. They may need the last word, they may need some form of validation from the interaction, they may even need their money back, but your greatest need – I urge you in the strongest possible terms – is to move on and get back to serving the 99.9 per cent of your customers and potential customers who actually deserve your time. Of course, you will be more easily able to move on if you take certain steps to protect your business, such as the use of electronic delivery confirmation, a good packaging system, order confirmation emails, judicious use of the Amazon A-to-Z Guarantee, and a conservative approach to rating and describing your books.

IV   Suppliers And Sources

The choices you make about where to get the supplies and services you need to run your business can make a difference of hundreds or even thousands of dollars in profit, and dozens of hours of working time, each and every year you are in business. If you are averaging 35 cents a book as your cost of acquiring inventory, you certainly wouldn't want to see that cost double, would you? Then why would you want to add 35 cents a book to your shipping cost by failing to get the best deal on mailer packaging, or another 38 cents a book by paying too much for delivery confirmation? These are just a few examples. Let's look one-by-one at the basic supplies and services you will need and some of the best ways to get them.

Shipping Carriers

The *United States Postal Service* (www.usps.com) wants your business, and you should give it to them because it is the best and cheapest way to make your shipments. Ongoing improvements and enhancements in USPS service mean that you can enjoy rates so cheap that you should actually make a small profit on Shipping & Handling, while getting your shipments delivered in a relatively quick time with the added assurance of Delivery Confirmation.

Most online booksellers take advantage of the inexpensive shipping rates available through the United States Postal Service's Media Mail and Priority Mail offerings, which also align themselves well with the shipping credits available on Amazon.com's Marketplace and eBay's Half.com. While online booksellers often experience anxiety about coming postal rate increases, Amazon and Half.com have proven to be very responsive so far in increasing shipping credits in conjunction with these hikes.

USPS Media Mail is advertised as taking 4 to 14 days, but often is delivered in 3 to 5 days, especially if the address includes the Zip+4 zip code, and it can now be enhanced with a Delivery Confirmation service (see Endicia services below). As of this writing, Amazon.com

Table 1: Making Shipping & Handling Credits Work for You

It's certainly possible to lose money on Shipping & Handling if a large percentage of the books you ship are heavier or larger than "the average." If you are shipping a lot of computer books, oversized hardcovers, or other cumbersome items, you will want to build an extra dollar or so into your item prices. Otherwise, if you are shipping a general stock of used paperback and hardcover books, there is frankly just no excuse for losing money on Shipping & Handling, and you may well make a small profit on it. As we go to press, we are still awaiting announcements from Amazon and Half.com regarding adjustments in shipping credits to reflect the USPS rate hike that will take effect June 30, 2002. The formulas below, then, are based on the conservative projections that Media Mail credits will be raised to $2.26 and that credits for Priority and International Mail will stay the same. Here are some guidelines to help protect your profitability from being eroded by Shipping & Handling over-runs.

	STANDARD SHIPPING	EXPEDITED SHIPPING	GLOBAL SHIPPING
Shipping credit	$2.26	$4.35	$8.95
USPS Rates			
Small flat envelope (less for Canada & Mex.)	N.A.	N.A.	$5.00
Large flat envelope (less for Canada & Mex.)	N.A.	$3.85	$9.00
(Weight limit for flats: 4 pounds)			
Package up to 1 pound	$1.42	$3.85	N.A.
Package up to 2 pounds*	$1.84	N.A.	N.A.
Package up to 3 pounds*	$2.26	N.A.	N.A.
1st Class Mail 5.1 to 6 oz.	$1.52	$1.52	N.A.
Electronic delivery confirmation	$0.12	$0.12	$0.00
Packaging	$0.30	$0.10	$0.10
Other shipping supplies: labels,			
tape, bubble wrap	$0.10	$0.10	$0.10

The following is based on the premise that, on average, out of 10 books you ship 1 will be under 6 oz., 4 will be 6-16 oz, 3 will be 1-2 lbs, and 2 will be 2-3 lbs; also, that that 2 out of 10 would fit in a small Global Priority Flat Envelope.

	STANDARD SHIPPING	EXPEDITED SHIPPING	GLOBAL SHIPPING
Average postage	$1.72	$3.85	$8.20
Average other costs	$0.52	$0.32	$0.20
Total average S&H expense	$2.24	$4.17	$8.40
Average S&H profit	$0.02	$0.18	$0.55

Naturally, this hypothetical breakdown of shipping weights will vary depending on what books you stock. But to make sure that you do not lose money on shipping, it is critically important never to select these shipping options for oversized books that will not fit in a Priority Mail Large Flat Envelope or Global Priority Large Flat, or to otherwise cover your cost by building any additional shipping costs into your pricing for items that do not fit into a flat.

and Half.com pass through to their sellers a Media Mail shipping credit equal to the cost of shipping a book that weighs up to 3 pounds, which means a slight additional profit for booksellers since most paperbacks weigh less than a pound and most hardcovers weigh less than 2 pounds. A higher credit is available if a seller offers the option of "expedited shipping" for Priority Mail or 1st Class Mail shipments and the buyer selects that option.

USPS also provides a fast and inexpensive way to make most international shipments through Global Priority Mail, for which there are pre-printed Flat Rate Envelopes that take about a week to arrive and currently costs $4 to $9 depending on package size and destination. The smaller Flat Rate Envelopes hold mass market paperbacks and smaller trade paperbacks, and cost only $4 to $5 to mail. The larger Flat Rate Envelopes, which cost $7 to $9 to mail, will hold a fairly large oversized hardcover. But remember that these envelopes are not padded and you should take additional padding steps to secure your shipment and make sure it arrives safely in the condition sent.

For all international book orders with stated value under $32 the customs form you will need PS Form 2976, a small green and white form about the size of personal check that you can pick up in some quantity at the post office. It takes about a minute to fill out, and under "value" many booksellers ordinarily estimate the value they paid for a book, usually a dollar or two, so as not to provide gratuitous customs and taxation issues for their buyer.

Get to know the staff at your local post office, letting them know what you do and exchanging courtesies whenever possible. If you handle things well they should allow you to bypass the counter line and bring your daily bin(s) directly to the front of the line without waiting, and they may also take helpful steps such as giving you a call to come back and correct an error rather than simply sending a package back to you in the mail.

The rates offered by the Postal Service's competitors such as **United Parcel Service** (www.ups.com) and **Federal Express** (www.fedex.com) are simply too high to present a compelling alternative to Media Mail rates, or even to Priority Mail, but a seller occasionally may want to use Federal Express when a customer sends an email stating his preference and is willing to provide his FedEx number so that the charges will be billed to his account.

Buying Postage Online

Several companies have emerged recently to provide "internet postage", which allows you the convenience of purchasing your postage online, printing and affixing your own postage labels, and thereby creating a more professional looking package while also achieving two important efficiencies: you can avoid standing in line at your local post office to buy stamps, and you can save a few cents a day by avoiding the mixing and matching of stamps to cover postage. Unfortunately, this is where I must tell faithful Macintosh users that, as I write this, I have yet to find an Internet postage service that supports the Macintosh operating system. So, if you are a Windows user and you opt for such a service, you'll pay a monthly service charge in the $10 to $20 range for the Internet service, and you will also have to buy special labels that will probably cost you between 5 and 10 cents per label. While we don't like standing in line to buy stamps, we've gone through periods of using old-fashioned postage stamps in part because we are aware of the fact that our stamp purchases help the local post office and its employees in the USPS budget process.

However, one of the newest internet postage enhancements tips the scales decisively in favor of using internet postage: *it is now possible to include a Delivery Confirmation option in the internet postage label that you can print right at your computer and affix to the package before leaving for the post office*. The cost is only 12 cents for Media Mail, or free for Priority Mail, compared to 50 cents if you purchase Delivery Confirmation at the post office window. Not only does this allow you peace of mind about whether and when a shipment will be received, but it also places you in a position to provide much greater peace of mind for your customer by sending a confirmation email message that includes that customer's Delivery Conformation number. These enhancements to shipping security and customer service are especially important given the postal security issues associated with the anthrax mailings in the Fall of 2001.

One of the newer vendors for Internet postage, called *endicia* (www.endicia.com), has incorporated the newest enhancements in a very user-friendly and inviting package that allows a business user to print extremely professional and visually striking labels that not only include the basics of postage, delivery confirmation, and return and ship-to addresses but also enhance your package with logo, graphics, and message mail – all of which is offered very inexpensively and with the lowest monthly service fee we have found among Internet postage vendors. But these services are likely to experience fierce ongoing competition and we recommend that you check out all of *endicia's* competitors as well, including *Stamps.com* (www.stamps.com), *Neopost's Simply Postage* (www.neopost.com), and Pitney Bowes' *Clickstamp* (www.pitneyworks.com).

Shipping Supplies and Equipment

Nothing against *Staples* – it's been one of my favorite places to shop for nearly 20 years and I have to run over there this afternoon to pick up a few things. But if you are depending on Staples for things like padded envelopes, tape, and bubble wrap, you are wasting a significant amount of folding money. The problem is not that Staples' prices are so bad; it's just that you can't get very good prices for padded envelopes if you are buying them one or two dozen at a time. We were lucky enough early in our business life to find a very inexpensive and responsive business-to-business supplier of packaging and shipping supplies, Associated Bag Company. Associated Bag provides first-order credit to new business customers, offers 30-day payment terms, and is accessible both online (www.associatedbag.com) and through traditional means of contact (Associated Bag Company, 400 West Boden Street, Milwaukee WI 53207-7120, Telephone: 800-926-6100, Fax: 800-926-4610). But most importantly, Associated Bag offers all the shipping and packaging supplies you will ever need at prices so low that you will save big money compared to Staples and other vendors even after paying shipping charges from the Associated Bag warehouses.

When buying from Associated Bag, try to plan and combine your orders for maximum discounting and shipping efficiencies. You'll also find that they understand your desire to keep shipping costs down and will be conscientious and communicative on that subject with you. We recommend that you use the products manufactured directly by Associated Bag whenever possible as their quality is top-shelf and their prices are of course lower than third-party products.

In order to keep it simple and avoid using too much simple and avoid using too much warehousing space for shipping supplies, we have refined our use of Associated Bag products to just six products, which include bubble wrap, clear packing tape, and four sizes of self-sealing padded manila envelopes:

- Item 132-922, which holds most mass market paperbacks, CDs, and the smallest of trade paperbacks;

- Item 132-924, just right for most trade paperbacks and some smaller hardcovers;

- Item 132-925, for most hardcovers; and

- Item 132-927 for oversize books and multiple-item shipments.

So, as you may have noticed, we can give Associated Bag a strong recommendation as a great source to meet your needs for shipping and packaging supplies, but don't just take our word for it. The continuing growth of businesses such as ours will certainly sustain continued fierce competition in the business-to-business market for shipping and packaging supplies, and we strongly recommend that you do an online search, every few months, under "shipping supplies" to see what is out there in terms of best deals and service.

Meanwhile, here are some other sources that have received good reviews from some booksellers:

- ULINE Shipping Supplies (www.uline.com)

- Hillas Packaging Network (www.hillas.com)

- Papermart (www.papermart.com)

Banking

If you haven't done so already, you should immediately set up a separate checking account for your business rather than using your personal checking account and commingling personal and business bank

TransparentMail

Another relatively new "packaging system" that has generated a great deal of buzz and very favorable reviews from online sellers is called *TransparentMail*, which is surprisingly inexpensive and appears to be aimed directly at the bookselling market and tailored to our special requirements. Here's the pitch from www.transparentmail.com:

"TransparentMail is a revolutionary method of shipping products to your customers. For years, businesses like yours have used cardboard boxes and bubble wrap, padded mailers, and bubble mailers to ship books, cd's, videos, dvd's, and more. These older methods are certainly not cheap and require a fair amount of storage space for the materials. TransparentMail utilizes bubblewrap or foam padding surrounded by durable plastic sleeves for materials, resulting in lower cost, lighter packages, less storage space and happy customers. Not only is the finished package waterproof, it is also airtight and tamper-proof. The finished package is extremely durable, and can endure rugged handling without damage to the contents. Our mailer material is also tear and rip resistant, unlike ordinary poly material."

activity. Once you establish separate accounts, be true to the separation. Use the business account to pay for your book, supply, and postage purchases and other business expenses, and don't use it to buy groceries. If you move money from your business account to your personal account, or use your business account to write a check for groceries, account for it as compensation or as an "owner's draw." Keeping bank accounts separate will make it a lot easier to make sense of how you are doing, and it will pay off in efficiency when it is time to summarize and organize your annual business records and file your tax returns.

It also makes a lot of sense to use a truly Internet-compatible online bank for your checking account services, in keeping with suggestions elsewhere in this book that you use the Internet to the greatest extent possible to run your business. Why? The nature of online bookselling calls for a large number of banking transactions including account credits on a daily basis for your sales revenue and shipping credits from Amazon.com, Half.com, payment processing services, and other bookselling websites, and multiple debits for your book, postage, and supply purchases as well as customer refunds and website service fees. Banking online will allow you to view your account with a few mouse-clicks and to see these credits and debits hit your account on a real-time basis so that you can manage your cash flow accordingly. Even more importantly, choosing a good online bank will allow you to download the full details of all your banking transactions directly onto your own computer in files compatible with programs such as QuickBooks, Quicken, and Excel. This will save you many hours when it comes time to summarize your annual business records and file your tax returns.

It's entirely possible that your favorite local brick-and-mortar bank has transformed itself sufficiently to meet your online business banking needs, and if that's true it makes good sense to bank there for all the traditional reasons why small business owners like to establish positive relationships with banks in the communities where they run their businesses, obtain their mortgages, buy their automobiles, and try to figure out how to get their kids through college. But if you feel the need to cast a wider net, or want to see how online banks stack up against each other, check out the Banking scorecard at www.Gomez.com. Gomez maintains scorecards that benchmark online banking performance in such areas as Ease of Use, Customer Confidence, On-Site Resources, Relationship Services, and Overall Cost. Two banks that seem to perform well consistently on these scorecards are Netbank (www.netbank.com) and First Internet Bank of Indiana (www.firstib.com).

In addition to check writing and online Bill Payment services, you should also make sure to get a Visa or MasterCard debit card linked to your business checking account. Don't get a credit card, which could put unnecessary pressure on your business, but a debit card that will allow you to make online purchases such as books and Internet postage and have them automatically charged to your business. When it comes time to prepare your taxes you don't want to be hunting down scraps of paper to tally up your business expenses, so every system you can set up now to streamline things then will end up saving you time and money. To the greatest extent possible, you should take advantage of these opportunities that will essentially allow you to run your business online. Such practices will be worth a great deal to you in streamlining the process of organizing and summarizing your annual business records and filing your tax returns. At the same time you allow yourself to depend on such conveniences, be sure to take the necessary steps to keep your computerized data secure, including making regular backups of all data and using an anti-virus program regularly to scan all files on your hard drive.

Accepting Credit Card Payments

If your bookselling is limited to Amazon.com and/or Half.com, the customers who make purchases from you will be able to use credit cards easily by making payments directly to Amazon or Half.com without any concern about giving their credit card information to an unknown entity. The transaction fee that you pay to Amazon or Half.com will include their percentage for processing the payment, and the money will flow automatically into your account (usually in about five days with Amazon, but in two to four weeks with Half.com).

However, you may wish to establish your own independent ability to accept credit card payments directly from customers for one of the following reasons:

- To allow you to sell books through your own website;

- To allow you to make special sales directly to customers; or

- To allow you to accept credit card payments directly on a site such as eBay or an independent bookseller database such as Advanced Book Exchange (www.abebooks.com) that allows sellers to set up their own means for accepting payments.

Many booksellers are happy to accept buyer payments through **PayPal** (www.paypal.com), which can provide an easy and seamless experience for both buyer and seller, is used by over 2 million businesses, and handled $3.5 billion in transactions in 2001. Basically PayPal allows buyers and sellers to exchange instant, secure payments with one another using their existing checking accounts and credit cards. Transaction fees can be as low as 2.2% plus 30 cents per transaction. You can easily set up an account and accept payments either by email or directly on your website, so it makes good sense to set up a PayPal account and use it whenever possible. With all of the good things about PayPal, there's just one catch: a buyer has to establish a PayPal account in order to be able to make a payment, and unfortunately there are millions of online book buyers who have never heard of PayPal. As a retailer dealing with a buyer for the first time, you don't necessarily want to be in the position of trying to persuade the buyer to try out an unknown system for paying you (although if you succeed at such persuasion PayPal may send you five dollars). If you are planning on using PayPal, let me err on the side of an "abundance of caution" (I hate it that I have borrowed this phrase from Rudy Giuliani) and suggest that you may want to take a look at www.PayPalWarning.com, a complaint board about PayPal. While you may get a sense of potential problems to avoid, and how to deal with them if they do occur, I should also be clear that I have heard far more positive reviews than negative, from booksellers, about PayPal.

Another option available to booksellers is an exciting and relatively new one called **ProPay** (www.propay.com). A privately held Utah company founded by Brad Wilkes in 1997, ProPay has partnered with payment processing companies to allow individuals and very small businesses to accept direct credit card payments with an extremely low fee structure in a variety of ways including face-to-face, online, over the telephone, and via email or PDA. ProPay charges a $35 one-time setup fee with normal transaction fees of 3.5% plus 35 cents per transaction.

Quickbooks Merchant Account Service (www.quickbooks.com/services/mas/more.html) also offers a competitive small business program through Chase with charges of $9.95 plus 2.35% of all transactions and a 20-cent-per-transaction processing fee. By comparison, many booksellers are charged several hundred dollars a year for traditional bank merchant credit card services, with transaction fees ranging from 4% to as high as 9.9%!

Internet and Email Connections

In choosing the Internet Service Provider (ISP) to meet your business' needs, it's worth paying special attention to two issues, *connection speed* and *accessibility:*

• *Connection speed* is important in posting your books online, especially if you are posting them one at a time on Amazon, where each manual book listing requires about half a dozen screen views and connection speed can make the difference between being able to post a dozen books in an hour and four times that many. Monthly fees for a cable modem or DSL connection are usually higher than those for a standard 56K modem connection, but the difference in fees may be tiny compared to the difference in sales that you could experience by speeding up the process of posting your books online. That being said, in the interest of full disclosure, I should acknowledge that I live in a town that is still waiting for cable internet access and I've made do very well with a 56K connection, partly by adding RAM to speed up our computer's CPU.

• By *accessibility,* I mean the ability to connect to our internet account when we travel. We maintain an AOL account all the time partly because of the nearly universal geographical access to AOL via local access numbers in any small town we might visit.

Even if I am on vacation and have made provision to have most orders turned "off" via the On-Off vacation switch at Amazon and Half.com, it is still very important to our business to be able to receive and respond to buyer's customer service issues and emails whenever they turn up.

But the decision about your ISP is separate from the decision about what email service and client to use. As a Cherokee Indian, I have non-business reasons for using an excellent email provider called Nativeweb (www.nativeweb.net), but regardless of those reasons, the features I get from Nativeweb are features I would be seeking if I were looking elsewhere for an email service.

Email messages are the day-to-day currency of our business, and it is essential to organize your email messages so that you don't lose essential information. In our business, we use email message filters and folders to achieve this kind of organization. For instance, for the email account that is linked to our Amazon.com seller account, we have organized the account into the following folders:

Folder	Messages
INBOX	0
Sent	143
Drafts	0
Trash	1
Spam	2
Amazon.com issues & misc.	47
Customer service follow needed	5
Customer service issues resolved	53
Sales emails, awaiting confirmation	17
Sales emails, confirmations sent	754

Whenever we receive an email message from "Amazon.com Payments," one of the filters we have created automatically diverts that message into the folder titled "Sales emails, awaiting confirmation." These messages, of course, are the ones that give us the go-ahead to ship an item because the buyer in question had completed his payment transaction with Amazon. All other incoming emails go to the Inbox, and we sort or dispose of them accordingly, but we don't want to take a chance on zapping one of these key sales email messages. Letting it sit with dozens of other messages in the inbox would be like leaving a $20 bill in a physical in-box with the mail, a few memos, the sports page, and miscellaneous other pieces of paper.

Speaking of $20, I should disclose here that, while a standard email account at Nativeweb is free, we pay about $20 a year for our Nativeweb email account so that we can have a large mailbox with more options including the "filtering" option that helps us sort our mail as it comes in, before we even see it. There are a variety of email vendors that provide such services in this price range, but one of the things we like about Nativeweb is that our outgoing email messages go out without any banners, nonsensical slogans such as "Do You Yahoo?," or other unwanted adornments. Also, given the fact that we exchange email messages with many previously unknown email partners daily, and we do not ask them their complete previous email history, we try to stay away from email clients or email management programs, such as Microsoft Outlook and Outlook Express, which have been targeted too frequently with email-carried virus attacks in the past couple years.

Inventory Software

There are several inexpensive Inventory Management software programs available for purchase, several others that are available free if you sign up for one of the databases that uses them, and one fundamental underlying question: do you really need such a program? In many cases, we suggest that the answer is "no," and that it makes more sense for you to do whatever you need to do to become proficient in using Microsoft Excel, which can serve as your central system brain and organizing tool for inventory (as well as fulfillment and sales), and can communicate just fine with most of the selling sites and listing services with which you are likely to come into contact. If you feel that you do need such a program, Abebooks provides a free database software program called Homebase, specifically designed with used, rare, and out-of-print booksellers in mind, which is free and downloadable from the Abebooks website at www.abebooks.com. Abebooks also has a free companion program for making price adjustments to existing inventory, and offers free technical support. It also makes sense to investigate Booktrakker (www.booktrakker.com) and BookHound and to do an online search for recent developments in this category.

Price Hunter

Another software package that bears watching is currently called Price Hunter and can be found at www.saveallsoft.com. Although it is currently hampered by poorly written documentation and some questionable decision-making in terms of promoting the product as fully launched when it was clearly in a pre-beta stage, the software itself creates a powerful user interface with Amazon's product pages and allows a seller to automatically bring up a wealth of useful information in sortable spreadsheet form for his entire inventory, including competitive prices, Amazon's price, sales ranking, condition and description of competitive listings, etc. This interface can then be edited with relative ease and used to upload or refresh a seller's inventory through Amazon's inventory loader. Price Hunter is currently priced at a one-size-fits-all $150 flat fee, but the pricing along with almost everything else about this package is "under discussion." It has the potential to be a powerful piece of software once they get their act together on documentation, marketing, pricing, name, and purpose. They should be marketing it as a tool for getting better prices, rather than for lowballing, and also as a tool for identifying titles for sellers to acquire.

The following information on Booktrakker and BookHound is provided by the Swiss-based *Bibliophile* listings service (www.bibliophile.net):

* **BookHound** is a book inventory, cataloguing and sales management system for out-of-print and antiquarian booksellers, which is built in FileMaker Pro and runs under Macintosh and Windows operating systems. A single user version costs US$150 and a customizable multi-user version US$275. Both versions have customer profile building, wants and consignment management, sales history, online searching, hard copy catalogue and index building, financial reporting, a built-in encyclopedia of over 400 bibliographic terms, and other features. Visit www.bookhound.net for more information and to download a fully functional demo version limited to fifty entries.

- **Booktrakker** is another book inventory, cataloguing and sales management system for used, out-of-print and antiquarian booksellers. It can be configured to upload UIEE files directly to selling venues at the click of a button. Visit www.booktrakker.com for demo and trial download.

This is probably also a good place to mention the existence of a service called BookRouter (www.bookrouter.com) that, for a fee, will handle all of your uploading, price adjustments, deletions, and other processing for as many selling venues as you wish to deal with. BookRouter charges a setup fee of $50 and a monthly fee of $25 for up to five sites, with an additional $5 on each fee for each additional site. BookRouter will work with virtually any software configuration a seller might use.

V   Building Your Inventory: Where To Get Books

Of all the possible issues in determining how well you might do in selling used books online, none is more critical than your ability to acquire uncommon, desirable books in very good condition. Not surprisingly, many sellers closely guard information about their sources of books, but the reality is that there is a great deal of information generally available on the subject and we are not giving away any deep dark secrets by pointing you in a few directions. The easy answer to the question "where do you find the books to sell?" does not provide much information, and yet it is telling: "Anywhere you can find them!"

As online bookseller Craig Stark proclaims in his excellent series on online bookselling in the AuctionBytes newsletter (www.auctionbytes.com), "Books are everywhere!"

Don't be too proud to search out some of the places enumerated below, but make some clear rules about the limits you are willing to pay for general stock and the quality of condition that must be met for you to buy a book, and stick to those rules. Here are some suggestions:

Library Sales. Also known as Friends of Library Sales or FOLs, these are held by hundreds of public libraries in every state in the country, and they are the most important single source for many and perhaps most sellers. An FOL sale may include library discards ("ex library" books, in our parlance), but it is also likely to include a wide range of other books donated by library patrons for the benefit of the library. An excellent source of online information about library sales is Book Sale Finder, viewable at www.booksalefinder.com. Not only can you click on any state to get all the details on upcoming sales, but you can also sign up for "Sale Mail" and they'll send you a weekly email message with information on all sales within a specified radius of your (or any) location. Book

Sale Finder also has several other services available including classified ads where you can list books for sale or items wanted.

While you are likely to get the biggest bumps in good inventory from the special occasion or regular monthly library sales you'll see listed by Book Sale Finder, you'll also help yourself out in the long run by identifying and regularly dropping in on the best "perpetual" library sales in your immediate area: libraries that put some of their donated books and/or discards out on the for-sale shelves on a more or less daily basis. It never hurts to make friends with the folks who staff or volunteer at these sales. While library staff have been known occasionally to show disdain for resellers by distinguishing them from "real readers", most people associated with library sales realize not only that that online resellers are the best thing that has ever happened to library book sales, but also that resellers shorten the process of getting books into the hands of the readers who really want them. In some cases I've found that cordial relationship with book sale volunteers has paid off with important information: "we'll be putting out a couple boxes of new things at about four o'clock Thursday afternoon."

Yard sales and ***garage sales*** are a fun way to spend time on weekend mornings, exploring nearby neighborhoods and exploiting a ready supply of books at bargain prices. You'll want to maintain your high standards for book quality while exercising your best bargaining skills to help the yard-salers see the benefit of saying goodbye to a larger quantity of books at a lower average price than what they tell you as walk up. Never be afraid to make an offer! I should point out here that I owe everything I am as a yard sale bargain hunter to my wife and her mother, who were filling their lives (along with their closets, attics, basements, and the trunks of their cars) with the fruits of their Saturday morning expeditions long before they knew me. I tended to refrain from and even perhaps disdain such activity until I began selling used books online, and now it has become one of the staple activities of our marriage.

Phantom yard sales. What are these? Well, I could have called this paragraph ***dumpster diving***, but I didn't want the elegance of this volume to suffer. Yesterday morning my wife got a call from a friend who lives a mile away. Her husband had just returned from a walk and noticed that a lot of books and other items, all seemingly in good condition, were packed up in front of a nearby home awaiting the weekly trash collection. My wife and three-year-old son and I were in the van 15 minutes later, and we returned another 30 minutes later, all having done quite well. Danny was very pleased, reaping a non-motorized scooter made by Honda and a Near Fine "Flexible Flyer" sled with only the slightest edge wear from gentle sledding, but I believe I did best of all, netting over 200 books, most of them in very good shape and most of them in the uncommon or scarce category, all for the price of 20 cents worth of gasoline and my time. It's not the first time I have happened upon such treasures, and certainly underscores the value of letting friends, family, and acquaintances know what we do so they can help scout for us. I have yet to get to the point where I drive the weekly trash routes in my town just after dawn, but if I were to suffer an inventory dearth I wouldn't hesitate for a minute.

Flea markets often have large book tables with good selections of hardcovers and paperbacks, but beware of getting into large collections of overstock or remaindered books that flea-market sellers may have purchased from jobbers directly for resale; these are often the titles that will swamp the online marketplace as well, so that you won't be able to sell them at a decent price. When you do see material that you want to buy, once again, don't be afraid to make a bargaining offer.

Thrift shops. Many thrift shops feature regular or perpetual sales along the lines of $5 for everything you can pack into a shopping bag, although sellers have noted a more recent trend toward higher thrift shop prices. This may well turn out to be a short-lived trend if market forces prevail, since sellers are unlikely to keep buying their inventory from any store if the prices make it unprofitable. Some of the best thrift shop sales we've found are not at the Goodwill and Salvation Army stores, but at the little church or hospital thrift shops that are open two days a week from 10 to 1. It makes sense to develop a list of these kinds of opportunity so you can keep coming back to them. Otherwise you'll be amazed at how many details you can forget! Or maybe that's just me.

Your personal library. A great many online booksellers are just selling books they originally purchased for their own use. Sometimes entrepreneurial sellers develop resentment toward these personal library sellers for silly things like not charging enough for their books, but it is worth remembering that these folks are also buyers, and whatever their "business practices," they play an important role both in building the overall marketplace and also in keeping the new book market fluid and its prices high, which at some level are important elements in maintaining a strong market for used books.

In any case, if you are the book lover that you ought to be if you are in this line of work, your personal library probably contains some good books, in very good condition, that would bring a nice price online. Some are books that you would never want to sell, but with others, keep two things in mind: first, you are going to be acquiring books by the hundreds every month that you are involved in this enterprise; and second, unless you are living either on a farm or at a more stratified economic level than most of us, you will eventually have to make some tough decisions about shelf space.

Other online used book dealers. If you have interest in the rare and antiquarian end of the used bookselling spectrum, I recommend that you become a member of The Bibliophile Mailing List (www.bibliophilegroup.com), a wonderful treasure trove that is maintained by Oregon bookseller Lynn DeWeese-Parkinson (www.bibliophilegroup.com/lynnsbookstore) for the benefit of sellers and/or collectors of rare, out-of-print, scarce books in all subject areas. Its subscribers include booksellers, librarians, students, scholars, and book lovers of all kinds. Participants will find books offered from a few dollars to many thousands of dollars. You will often find the pricing rather rich for almost anyone's blood, but there are occasional bargains and those doing the offerings include some of the most knowledgeable and experience booksellers anywhere. To subscribe to the Bibliophile Mailing List, send email to biblio-request@bibliophilegroup.com and put "subscribe" (without the quotes) in the body of your letter. At this writing there are dues of $30 per year.

Road trips. One of the true joys of being a used bookseller is the ability to plan trips to places near and far around your book acquisition efforts. If you plan your trip well, you'll be able to begin it with an itinerary of book sales and used bookstores that you can augment by keeping an eye out for thrift shops and other spots along the way, and end it by recording, documenting, and organizing the expenses deductions you'll be able to share with your Uncle Samuel come tax time.

Bookstores. Scout out all the used bookstores within a reasonable radius and decide which ones are worth stopping in on once a week, once a month, or once a year. While it is generally true that a retailer does not want to pay the prices implicit in acquiring most of his stock from other retailers, there are exceptions that are worth noting here. If a brick-and-mortar used bookshop does not sell online, there will usually be pricing discrepancies between its inventory and the normal range of online pricing, and as you gain experience and develop your ability to locate books that will fetch nice prices online, you will likely find that some of these volumes are occasionally hidden, and available on the cheap, in the darker recesses and back shelves of some used bookshops.

Even if a brick and mortar shop does sell online, the duties of maintaining a physical store and serving walk-in buyers and sellers are often very time-consuming and many such stores, because of the claims on staff time, have only gotten around to listing a small percentage of books online. In any case, the kind of treasure you may often find at a bargain price at such a store may be the out-of-place local interest book: for instance, Ruth Lee Webb's ***Sandwich Glass: The History of the Boston & Sandwich Glass Company*** will not last long if properly displayed in a Cape Cod bookshop, and always fetches anywhere from $20 to $150 depending on edition and condition if listed properly online, but if it turns up in a strictly brick and mortar bookshop in Milwaukee it may wait a good while before finding a buyer, and may consequently suffer in price and shelving location. So, if you are in Milwaukee, be on the lookout! More generally, wherever you are looking for books, realize that you are not constrained by location and gather up any cheaply priced volume that is likely to be desirable and scarce in nearly any village on the planet, because the miracles of modern science now allow you to open a bookshop simultaneously in nearly *every* village on the planet!

If, God forbid, you are at all like me and many of our bookselling colleagues, you probably enjoyed spending time in used bookshops long before you began selling, and it only makes sense to continue to indulge that pleasure now that you will also be making some purchases for resale. One difference between "now and then," of course, is that these days I usually enter a used bookstore with a small box of books "for trade" – items that for one reason and another I am not going to list online myself, but which I suspect will be staples for a brick and mortar shop – so that the likelihood of dispensing any actual folding money or leaving the store with a lightened wallet is greatly diminished. One thing to watch out for: a brick and mortar shop's "outdoor bargain" shelf or table may give you more than you bargained for if it is unprotected from the elements, because the ravages of dampness and critters (I believe that is the proper scientific term) are not always visible to the naked eye.

Half.com. Far more than Amazon.com, Half.com has experienced seller saturation without a concomitant influx of buyers, despite the fact that it is owned by eBay, one of the two largest e-commerce sites in the world. Early in its brief history Half.com imposed a price minimum of 75 cents for booksellers, so the result is that there are thousands of titles available for 75 cents, many of them described by their sellers as being in "Very Good" or "Like New" condition. Half.com charges its buyers far less than Amazon.com for shipping and handling, and consequently at this writing one can pick up any of these thousands of 75-cent titles for a total expenditure of $3.05. While it is true that I almost never pay as much as $3.05 for stock, there are a couple of situations which occasionally send me to Half.com for a book.

First, like every other volume seller online, I have occasionally experienced the embarrassment of selling a book from my listed online inventory only to find, when I go into the "pick and pack" mode, that the book is no longer there or is no longer in saleable condition. Maybe I gave it to one of my daughters and failed to delete its listing, maybe I managed somehow to list it twice by making a spreadsheet error, maybe I sold it on one venue and could not update my stock because of another venue's maintenance problems (yes, colleagues, I am being discreet here), maybe I tucked a paperback too tightly onto a shelf so that a cover became newly damaged, or, and I'm not saying this could ever happen, maybe my inventory organization needs a little attention. The first thing I do if I cannot ship a copy from stock is to check Half.com to see if there is a suitable copy from a highly rated seller available there. If so, I have it drop-shipped to my customer and I send the customer a brief explanation of what to expect. The customer has a good buying experience (I have done this perhaps 15 times in the past four years without a single complaint), and I still have a profitable transaction.

The other thing that I often do with Half.com is to check its pricing and availability for a title either when I list the title elsewhere or when I sell it from another venue. I have frequently found instances where it will make sense to replenish my stock from Half.com, although one would expect the potential for this kind of arbitrage profit to continue to diminish as the world of online bookselling becomes more and more populous and, one would think, more and more transparent. But a regular instance of this keeps occurring with the 1970s and 1980s self-help best-seller *Love and Addiction* by Archie Brodsky and Stanton Peele, which always seems to have very good copies available at Half.com for under a dollar while it continues to have a lowest available price of $7 to $8 at Amazon's Marketplace. I don't have any idea why this is true, but I am happy to assist in the process of making the market more efficient by buying copies at Half.com and selling them on Amazon. The key, of course, is to make sure you enter the transaction with a quality copy, a trustworthy seller, and sound arithmetic.

Since we are practically on the subject here anyway, this seems the right place to venture into the swampland of what many of our Amazon colleagues refer to as "drop-ship scams." If you peruse the listings very long in Amazon's Marketplace, you are likely to find a great many listings at wildly inflated prices by a few "sellers" who apparently do not actually stock many of their listed books themselves. You will often find that their storefronts contain somewhat confusing and convoluted references to "consignment", and if you read through their customer feedback files you will often find many references to titles that were not available, not shipped, not the edition ordered, or drop-shipped from another seller. The overall customer feedback rating is likely to be much lower than the average seller's rating of 4.6 or 4.7. At least one such seller is, according to the claims of other Amazon Marketplace sellers who have done considerable detective work on the subject, a teenager working out of his bedroom, not even old enough to enter into a binding contract. Whatever he may lack in age and ethics, he appears to compensate for in technical acumen and greed, since he appears to employ some sort of software "bot" which lifts other sellers' book descriptions verbatim and reprices them 500 per cent or so higher than the pilfered listings. Many sellers have reported receiving drop ship orders from this seller for books that he had listed at several times the market price. It is so difficult to figure out why any buyer would purchase a book for $95, when identical copies are available for $17.50 from sellers with much higher customer feedback ratings, that I have sometimes wondered if something publicly unspecified was included in the transaction. In any case, it is important to note that Amazon requires that a seller must have an item "on hand" at the time he lists it online, so sellers may want to think twice before agreeing to drop-ship their inventory for another seller if they have any reason to question that seller's business practices.

Estate sales. If you think a good Friends of Library sale is a competitive and cutthroat place, wait until you get to a good estate sale! For many sellers who have moved decisively beyond general stock and into the arena of scarce, rare, and antiquarian book sales, estate sales are their bread and butter, and often their *sine qua non*. When an affluent and well-read elderly person dies and leaves behind his library of a lifetime, there will often be books of significant value in the estate. For the individual's heirs or estate liquidators, the process of researching and pricing a large library individually is dauntingly labor-intensive, which often leads to bargain pricing at estate sales. Of course, some estate sales are better than others, and those in college towns are often the best.

If you are going to try to make a living from estate sale acquisitions, plan on arriving early, working in a very efficient and professional way, and weathering a few sharp elbows along the way. Take books off the shelves quickly and get them into a box or basket, then you can take a moment or two to peruse them and see if they make your final cut before actually approaching the cashier to make your purchases. Courtesy is contagious in the long run – sometimes the *very* long run – so have the good manners to return the other books to the shelves before you cash out.

Before you allow yourself to get totally swept up in a buying frenzy, a word to the wise from an esteemed colleague who employs a straightforward strategy for stretching her bookbuying dollar: "We go to estate sales on Saturday to look around and maybe grab the best of the best, then go back on Sunday and can walk away for at most half the Saturday price. It's win some-lose some, but sometimes it has to be that way."

You can find notices of estate sales in the classified listings of your metropolitan daily and local weekly newspapers, including shoppers' weekly papers. But don't stop there. Professional estate liquidators are good at what they do, and they and you have a definite mutual interest in getting to know each other. Keep a file of the contacts you make at sales and in perusing the listings, give them your business card, and begin to build relationships with them. Now and then one of them may come across small collections of books that for one reason or another he does not deem worthy of funneling into a public sale, and you, of course, would like nothing better than to get a call asking you if you would like to look those books over and make an offer.

Estate liquidators also are more and more likely to have an online presence for announcing their sales, marketing their services to potential clients, and providing generic information about estate sales. These sites can be enormously beneficial to you, most of all of course if they actually lead you to some good estate sales. The trick is to search for them online without pulling up every "real estate" listing in the universe, and the solution is to do a search on Google (www.google.com) with this highly complex search phrase: "**estate sales -real**". Putting the minus sign before the word "real" will opt you out of most of those real estate listings. Once you've looked over a few pages of the results of this search phrase, which just turned up 415,000 entries in 0.16 seconds when I entered it a moment ago, you may want to refine it by adding a geographical descriptor or two.

Special contacts. If you love movies as much as I do and are old enough either to shave or to associate with menfolk who shave other than your parents, you may recall an absolutely wonderful, if painful, scene from Paul Newman's great performance in *The Verdict*. Set in a real place, Spencer's Funeral Home on East Broadway in Southie, Newman's down and out non-recovering alcoholic gets bounced out of the funeral parlor onto the street for shamelessly working one too many wakes and trying to palm off his business card to the bereaved in hopes of getting some ambulance-chasing cases. Without suggesting that you start attending wakes, I do suggest that – if you really want to pursue rare, scarce, and antiquarian books and you've taken to heart the preceding paragraphs on estate sales – you can much more subtly emulate the basic strategy Newman's character employs. In addition to estate liquidators, the bereaved as a matter of course come into contact with undertakers and with clergy. If you live and work in a small town atmosphere and can find acceptable ways to make yourself and your enterprise known in a lighthanded way to either or both groups in your town, you may find that some day down the road one of them will mention you to a family member who has just offhandedly mentioned the need to get rid of a collection of books. Maybe this will happen, and maybe it won't, but my hope is that if you consider making these contacts the thought process will help to get you thinking in a more entrepreneurial way about the book acquisition side of your business, and that mode of thinking is the real secret to success.

Advertising for books. If you are regularly checking the newspapers for listings of yard sales and estate sales, you have no doubt noticed an occasional "Cash Paid for Books" advertisement, presumably for one of your competitors. In thinking about whether to place such an ad yourself from time to time, the key determinant is once again based on what kind of inventory you are trying to acquire. If you are trying to stock and sell general stock used books, it is very important to keep your operating costs to a bare minimum, and you should only consider placing an ad if you really have hit the wall in the normal processes of buying your stock at library sales, yard sales, and all of the other types of venues mentioned in this chapter. If that's the case, give it a try, but pay special attention to finding cheap or even free advertising rates. On the other hand, if you are seeking rare and scarce titles and have established your capacity to market and sell them well, placing such an ad makes great sense. Keep your ad brief and to the point: you have only one agenda in it, not several.

Surplus book jobbers. There are a fair number of book distributors that operate by buying remainder, overstock, or surplus copies in bulk from publishers or large bookstore chains at very low prices and reselling them to booksellers at deep discounts, usually in the 60 to 80 per cent range. My favorite jobber in this category has always been Daedalus Books (www.daedalus-books.com), whose very apt slogan is "Remainders for Readers." Daedalus has a wonderful selection of remainders – a tad different from what you find at the local "Buck a Book" – and describes itself thus:

"Since 1980 Daedalus Books has been the premier source for bibliophiles looking for quality books at bargain prices. From the thousands of books offered by publishers as remainders every year, we selectively choose books that are of lasting value. Remaindered books are the difference between what a publisher printed and what was sold. Bestsellers, classics, and overlooked gems get remaindered when the remaining stock is larger than the projected future sales. We are devoted to keeping these good books before the reading public. All of our books are hardcover editions (unless noted otherwise), and all are in good condition."

Daedalus offers booksellers a further 50 per cent discount off its deeply discounted listed prices, provided that the bookseller has a valid tax identification number and orders at least $200 at retail ($100 wholesale) in each order. Bookseller orders are charged actual shipping costs by Daedalus.

There are two problems that one should keep in mind, however, before getting into the business of selling remaindered books.

First, quite frequently there will be a glut in the online market of remaindered editions, and this is more and more likely to occur as the remainder outlets set up shop themselves on Amazon and elsewhere. It's one thing to wait for prices to stabilize if there are one or two lowballers each offering a single copy at extremely low prices, but it's another to deal with price competition from a seller who has 50 copies of a title in stock. One can easily research these conditions, of course, but it's important to be prepared for daily changes.

Second, the price vs. cost structure of your business is likely to be rather different for remaindered books than it is for the books you are picking up at library sales and yard sales for a dollar or less. With Daedalus, for instance, a book with a retail list price of $29.95 may be listed at $7.98, so that a bookseller's price is $3.99, and you may find that the online price the market for the title is around $15 to $18. Sounds great, but remember that you have to pay incoming shipping & handling costs and transaction fees, and then wait for the title to sell. Slow inventory turnover may not seem like much of a problem when you are averaging 40 cents a title purchased from yard sales, but your cash flow can suffer mightily once your costs escalate.

Auctions. Physical, real-world auctions that deal in used and antiquarian books tend to attract experienced dealers who are well equipped to deal with the natural competitive structure of an auction, so the advice here is to proceed with great caution. You may have fun and do well, however, at small-town, out-of-the-way auctions where the buying competition is not so decidedly professional. We are also aware that many online sellers acquire inventory in lots that are being auctioned off on eBay, but please remember that anyone who can sell such a book on eBay can sell it on Half.com or Amazon, so, again, proceed with caution: another seller's deadwood may become your deadwood. Personally I have heard stories of great success and also of great woe among those who have sought to acquire inventory online. Make sure that you have a good sense of four things:

- wholesale price structure you will need to be profitable;

- exact amount you will charged for shipping and handling;

- condition of books on which you might making a bid; and

- title and edition content and likely desirability of the lot on which you are considering making a bid.

The town dump. Well, we all have our dirty little secrets, don't we? In certain small New England towns the town dump is the special preserve of the true natives, a place where people gather on Saturday mornings to talk the real talk while the newcomer wannabes gather at Starbucks, and in a few of these towns there's a little building at the dump where people leave everything from furniture to books to tricycles, for the next guy to pick up if he is interested. I would never let on to my buyers that I was ever interested, because there are some things that I figure people just don't want to know. But I do know how to get to the dumps in more towns than I should probably admit to, and I also know enough never to go when my sinuses are blocked, because this particular source of used books tends to require special attention to what I will call the "sniff" test.

A Creative Bulletin Board Strategy. Here's a reward for reading through to (nearly) the end of this chapter: an extremely low-cost method for generating a significant influx of good used book inventory directly to you from your surrounding community. The idea is intended as a kind of online shopkeeper's substitute for the walk-in used book traders who have always been a big part of the bread and butter for brick-and-mortar used bookstores, but it has the added benefit of allowing you to participate in and encourage community-building and to create good will among men, women, and children. The first step is simple and straightforward: Use your computer to print up a dozen or so index cards like the one below and place them on as many community bulletin boards as you can find in your town, including schools, libraries, churches, community centers, laundromats, etc. Even better, if your community is graced with a college or university, or a hospital, search out the best bulletin boards available, especially in their libraries or in the buildings such as departmental offices where there may be faculty bulletin boards:

TURN YOUR USED BOOKS INTO *CASH*
FOR YOUR SCHOOL, CLUB, LIBRARY,
OR COMMUNITY GROUP!

Windwalker Books, a Belmont-based business, will accept your used books and make a 10% cash contribution based on their resale value to the school, club, or community organization of your choice. Books must be in very good condition without mildew or significant damage or wear.

FOR MORE INFORMATION
OR TO SCHEDULE A DONATION,
CALL 617-555-1287 TODAY!

At the same time you are doing this, it is very important to make some policy decisions and to then apply them consistently:

- Will you pick up books on location, or require that they be delivered to you?

- Will you be taking the tax deductions involved, or allowing the person providing the books to make the deductions?

- How will you respond if private citizens call to say they would like to give you a box of books and have you make the donation to *them*?

- Are there any exceptions to the range of organizations to which you will make donations? Will you require that such organizations be restricted to those who can provide you with an IRS letter showing that donations to them are tax deductible? (It is worth noting here that such status may not be necessary for you to take a tax deduction if the payment you are making is a purchase payment for inventory).

• Will you be using a phone number that actually rings in your home? This is important because most online booksellers working from home have grown pleasantly accustomed to a home life with relatively few intrusions from the business world, and the change can be jarring!

• How and when will you make the donations? One suggestion would be to tell the person who brings the books that you will list the books online within one week and that you will send a check on to that person, by specified date, to be delivered to the charitable organization in question. The check of course would be made payable to the organization. (On the other hand, as you will see below, you may want to establish a rule whereby you make the first contribution to any organization directly to that organization, so that you can establish ongoing institutional contact.)

• Will you pre-qualify the books on the telephone before either you or the initial contributor does any schlepping? Naturally such pre-qualification is far from fail-safe, but if you ask a few questions on the front end about selection and condition it will be easier for the donor to understand later why you don't want to take his books.

As you can see, the issues are potentially complex, but you will simplify them greatly if you resolve the policy issues on the front end and apply them consistently. If you try this inventory-building strategy and the first two or three contributors don't really contribute anything of value, don't be too quick to give up on the strategy. Over the long haul you will often find that a significant percentage of the folks who contact you will have books that you will be very happy to get.

As we hinted above, there is also another possible tier of activity here, wherein some of the organizations involved could decide to use your idea (you bought this book, so you can call it "your" idea) as *an ongoing institutional fundraiser.* That's why I suggested above that, the first time you have a donation for the Cesar Chavez Middle School, you may want to make a phone call to the principal and make an appointment to bring it over yourself so that you can establish initial contact and introduce the possibility of an ongoing fundraiser where the school (or club or civic group) actually encourages its members to get their old books to you or even holds a book drive! It could happen. But if it does, be prepared to lay out some cash, just as you would expect to do at a good library sale or an estate sale.

Along similar lines, you may also find it worthwhile to *send out an email version* of the index card message if you can get your hands on useful email lists or directories such as the local university's faculty email list. If you use email, make sure you lead with the philanthropic nature of your mission so as to reduce as much as possible the number of recipients who will be turned off because they think of your message as "spam."

We'd love to see used booksellers in every town or neighborhood in the United States carry out this strategy. Yes, we do have ulterior motives. In addition to the fact that this strategy should allow you to pre-empt the ultimate movement of many good used books to your competitors who would otherwise have an equal chance to get them at library sales, yard sales, etc., it should also reduce somewhat the number of people in your town who are likely to sell a few books here and there online without ever becoming entrepreneurial about it. While we have nothing against people selling a few books here and there on Amazon or Ebay or Half.com, because ultimately it does increase overall book-buying tendencies, we also think that it's a good thing for each of these online marketplaces if the vast majority of the transactions on these venues involve sellers who understand professionalism, customer service, and the terminology and standards of the used bookselling profession, and take them very, very seriously.

What should you pay for your inventory? In 1986 a colleague by the name of Dale L. Gilbert wrote a terrific guide to running a brick and mortar used bookshop (***Complete Guide to Starting a Used Bookstore***, Chicago Review Press, 0-914091-89-1), which has gone out of print and become fairly scarce and expensive. In it he provided some good rules of thumb for buying (and trading for) general stock brought into a brick and mortar store, and these formulas were based on the idea that a store would sell used books for half their cover price (adjusted for inflation, of course), buy them from customers for one-fourth what the store intends to sell them for, and or take them in trade for double that amount. So, if a customer brings in a nice paperback copy of *The Firm* for $7.95, then you would expect to receive $3.95 for it, and you would offer your customer $1 in cash or $2 in trade.

Sadly, things have changed. At this writing, there are 674 copies of The Firm for sale on Amazon's Marketplace, and 48 of them are priced at one penny each. If you buy many such books at a dollar each you'll be out of business very soon, unless you have a brick and mortar shop which may or may not provide a way of selling titles that have become cheaper than paper online. The general stock sellers who are operating profitably online are acquiring the vast majority of their books at a far lower cost, often averaging less than a quarter a book overall, and they are avoiding glutted or deadwood titles like the plague. My own rules of thumb for maximum general stock prices is one dollar for hardcovers, fifty cents for trade paperbacks, and twenty-five cents for mass market paperbacks. I'll make an exception maybe once for every two hundred general stock titles I pick up, or if I see a book I want to read first, or if I am using trade credit at a brick and mortar used bookstore. But keep in mind that those rule of thumb prices are maximums, and when I attend a good Friends of Library sale I am usually looking to acquire good stock for an average price of 15 to 20 cents per book.

VI   What Books To Get

Selecting books for resale on the Internet has become more and more difficult in a very short time. As recently as October of 2000, one could post a nice hardcover copy of Barry Sears' *The Zone* online for $15 and be virtually guaranteed it would sell within 48 hours. Best-selling mass market paperbacks could be sold quickly for half their cover price, or $3.75, and popular trade paperbacks would bring $7 to $10 with rapid turnover.

Not any more. In March 2002 there are 137 copies of *The Zone* available on Amazon's Marketplace and 417 available at Half.com; the market for a very good copy of the book on Amazon is under $8, and on Half.com it is under $3. The best selling mass market paperbacks are selling for a penny on Amazon and the 75-cent minimum at Half.com, and many very good, popular trade paperbacks have seen their online price market fall to the $1 to $4 range.

Yet despite these signs of market saturation in some titles, many sellers are doing just fine selling books online. What's their secret? It's definitely not a matter of ignoring the downward price spirals and listing the same books at higher prices in hopes that buyers will rise to meet them. Dream on.

No, the secret is no secret at all. The successful sellers are the ones who manage to find books that are still relatively uncommon or scarce and get them inexpensively. Are we talking rare? No. Rare and antiquarian books certainly continue to have a flourishing market, but it can be a tough market to buy in, because there is a lot of competition from other, very savvy book dealers.

A New Set Of Categories

In order to make the point a little more clearly, let's come up with a new set of categories for used books: ***hyper-common, outdated, common, uncommon, scarce,*** and ***rare***. Here's what we can say about each of these somewhat arbitrary categories. (But bear with me as I try to provide anecdotal examples of each category, because the specifics are bound to change very quickly, and the particular titles, sales rankings, and price markets cited here will be — speaking of **outdated** — yesterday's news).

Hyper-common books are books that have already saturated the new-book market with huge printings based on the guaranteed sales associated with names like John Grisham, Tom Clancy, Danielle Steel, Nora Roberts, and Stephen King or with the imprimatur of an Oprah selection or perhaps even a mention by Don Imus. As used mass market paperbacks, their retail price market is usually less than a dollar, and sometimes less than a dime, and is likely to stay there, with occasional exceptions. Nice trade paperback versions may bring as little as a dollar or two, and most hardcover copies won't bring much more. One kind of exception is that there will often remain a pretty good market for very good to fine first edition hardcovers in fine dustjackets, provided that they are listed as collectibles. Amazon's Marketplace condition and category structure allows these fine or near fine modern first editions to be sold as collectible at a minimum price one penny above the list price for the book, so that a "collectible" first edition of Grisham's **The Partner**, for instance, can be listed at any price from $26.96 up. So, it's worth picking up such modern first editions if they are in very good or better condition, but otherwise stay away from hardcovers, trade paperbacks, and mass market paperbacks in this category.

While I have focused on fiction authors as the easiest examples of hyper-common books, there are plenty of non-fiction examples. We found 276 trade paperback copies of Stephen Covey's **The Seven Habits of Highly Effective People** available on Amazon's Marketplace, with a market price under $5, when the book was ranked in the top 100 in new book sales. There's a market glut beginning to happen, and in all likelihood the used book price will dip down to a dollar or so when demand tapers off a bit or a revised edition hits the shelves. In addition to heavily sold business titles, another category that seems to saturate the market is books by comedians. Books by very funny people like Bill Cosby, Jerry Seinfeld, Paul Reiser and Ellen DeGeneres are obviously helpful in complementing the meager day-job earnings of their authors, but in most cases they won't do much for your earnings.

The economics of the publishing industry work very differently for fiction than for non-fiction. Of the more than 125,000 new titles published institutionally each year, fewer than 10 per cent are fiction. Of these fiction titles, the overwhelming majority of **actual copies printed** are novels, mysteries, and romances by a relatively small number of authors whose track record has made them guaranteed best sellers. Publishers spend huge marketing budgets on them, and they tend to pay off not only with big hardcover sales but also by selling the rights to the mass market paperback editions, the trade paperback editions, the book club editions, the audio book editions, the films, the film tie-in editions, and the foreign editions. These books begin with six- and seven-figure print runs, become hypercommon, and their used copies glut the online markets.

Non-fiction books and fiction books by novelists who have not proven themselves best sellers, on the other hand, tend to get much smaller print runs and marketing budgets. In the case of non-fiction how-to books, they also tend to be coveted by people who desire the specific expertise available between their covers, which means that they tend to hold their value if they are not over-printed or outdated. One important exception to watch out for involves non-fiction books that go through regular revisions. For instance, the 1997 mass market paperback edition of Dr. Atkins New Diet Revolution was one of Amazon's top self-help best sellers in 2001 and would probably still be good for two or three bucks used, but for the fact that Dr. Atkins came up with some new things to say (we assume) and published a "Revised and Improved" mass market paperback edition in December 2001. As a result, at this writing a few months later there are 334 copies of the older and less improved edition available on Amazon's Marketplace, with half a dozen listed at a penny and dozens more listed at less than four bits. A similar dynamic, of course, is usually at work with computer books, especially software guides that have the potential to make you dizzier than Dan Rather in a West Texas twister if you start trying to keep

72

track of whether version 5.1 or 7.7 or 2001 is the most current software available.

But probably worst of all, among outdated books with which you will want to avoid spinning your wheels, are previous editions of textbooks. It has likely happened to every new and hopeful book dealer: you find a big, thick, heavy, pristine textbook, printed in 1999, at a library sale or garage sale for a buck. The list price is $72.50 and you can't wait to get it home to offer it to some poor, starving student for the bargain price of $36.25! But when you go to list it you learn there is just one small problem – there's a new edition just printed, so your only chances at selling it will be either (a) to hope that some dunce will get the edition wrong and buy your copy, with the likely result that the kid will get in trouble for having the wrong edition and then come back to you sheepishly, at best, apologizing for his mistake and asking for a refund; or (b) listing it fraudulently as if it is the new edition, which will definitely lead to a refund request that will be anything but sheepish! Truth is, I usually pick up good-looking relatively recent textbooks when I find them for a buck or less, because if one out of four is a current edition and I donate and deduct the other three, it's a significant net gain.

Common books are titles that will always be readily available to the online buyer because they were heavily printed, but they are not so ubiquitous that you'll find dozens of very good copies available for less than a dollar each. Chances are you can make money on them – an average of two to five dollars per sale for paperbacks -- but not enough to thrive at your business if they are the only things you are selling. Buy them when can get them for a quarter apiece, but adhere to very strict condition standards of "Very Good" or better. Popular non-fiction books often fit this category, especially self-help and recovery titles, but when I try to think of examples one group that comes to mind involves what I will call older contemporary serious fiction such as the works of J.D. Salinger, May Sarton, Doris Lessing, John Fowles, Ken Kesey, Saul Bellow and the pre-1980 works of John Updike, Philip Roth, and Larry McMurtry. Another group whose books are common includes some of my own favorite contemporary writers such as Richard Ford, Toni Morrison, Carl

Hiaasen, and Sue Miller who are commercially successful but not at the megastar level of the Kings and the Clancys. Finally, one group of common books for which there will always be reasonably good demand are the classics of college literature courses by authors such as Dostoyevsky, George Eliot, William Faulkner, and so forth.

Uncommon books are probably where you'll make your money, the more so as you develop your instincts for what to buy. They are not to be found in every single brick-and-mortar bookshop you will ever enter and, while there some copies available online, there are few enough that there is relative balance between supply and demand and the price has not spiraled downward. On the other hand, these books are not by any means scarce, and it is doubtful you will sell them with inflated prices. The price market for very good used copies is likely to be somewhere near or just slightly below half of the current list price. Among fiction authors, for just about any popular author, you will find examples of titles that are hyper-common, common, and uncommon:

- Most of Robert B. Parker's Spenser, Jesse Stone, and Sunny Randall novels, along with a few other books like **Poodle Springs** and **All Our Yesterdays**, are hyper-common or common and have online price markets, for very good used copies, ranging from a penny to, say, $1.50. Parker's very interesting and somewhat eccentric early novel **Love and Glory** has tended to be uncommon, with a price market in the $3.50 to $5 range, although the price may have dipped by as much as a dollar recently. The 1994 coffee table book **Spenser's Boston** on which Parker collaborated with photographer Kasho Kumagai is scarce, though far from rare, and its price market hovers around $100.

- Some of the Toni Morrison novels that have seen numerous book club edition printings, such as **Jazz, The Bluest Eye,** and **Song of Solomon**, were hyper-common for a while and their price markets dipped ell below a dollar. However, very interestingly, they have recovered somewhat to the $1 to $3 range more recently, so that I would rank them as common and note that this regrouping seems to suggest some growing bookseller savvy about avoiding market gluts until prices have stabilized a bit.

- Morrison's *Sula* has just been named an Oprah selection, and perhaps Oprah's last selection, at this writing, and one can therefore expect that for several months its will be uncommon and its price market will rise toward the $5 to $10 range, after which it will fall dramatically as the truckloads of copies purchased after Oprah's anointing will hit the used market and become common again.

- As I write this, the phenomenal early success of Rebecca Wells' debut novel ***Divine Secrets of the Ya-Ya Sisterhood***, which later led to its availability for pennies on Amazon Marketplace, is being recapitulated as a result of the marketing campaign for a film version. After it made my list of titles that I would not acquire even for 25 cents because of the online glut, this title has risen again to Amazon's top 20 in sales rankings, and the price market for a very good paperback copy is back up to the $7 to $8 range.

If you are going to buy and sell used fiction, your success will depend a lot on your ability to absorb this kind of information and develop a feel for the careers of well-known and lesser-known writers so that you can make educated guesses at first sight as to whether their books are common, uncommon, or scarce. I personally can't imagine anyone succeeding in this field without being a serious reader and a lover and student of literature, but maybe that's just my defensive bias because I need to make something, anything, out of that nicely bound degree in English Literature that's collecting dust in the attic.

Three favorite areas of mine, when it comes to finding uncommon books that will fetch a good price, are modern poetry books, large-print hardcovers, and library discards:

- By modern poetry books, of course, I am not speaking of anthologies but of the smallish editions, often in paperback, of relatively little-known poets. Books of poetry tend to be printed in very small print runs of 5,000 or fewer copies, and by definition they are uncommon and relatively immune to market gluts.

• Yet they regularly turn up on the perpetual sale shelf at my local library, and usually bring $10 to $30 online. If I put such a volume on the shelf at a brick and mortar store and did not market it anywhere else, it might sit for five or ten years. But the wonderful thing about selling such a book online is that it only takes one buyer from the tens of millions to whom one has access.

• Large print hardcovers are printed in relatively small print runs, as well, and the people who are looking for them really want them. Virtually all of the large print books I have ever acquired have been library discards priced at a

---

Don't Buy These Books! Things to Avoid

There will be exceptions to nearly all of these prohibitions, but you'd better know why you are making exceptions before you make them!
• Book club editions
• Reader's Digest editions
• Outdated editions of textbooks
• Outdated editions of computer books
• Encyclopedias
• Popular romance mass market paperbacks
• Mass market editions of the highest selling books in the past two or three years
• Books with a musty odor, regardless of how clean they may look – mold and mildew spread!
• Outdated editions of extremely popular self-help books
• Books with broken hinges, missing pages, shaken spines or torn covers
• Books whose covers have been torn off – they are stolen goods
• Advance reading copies, unless "collectible"
• Hardcover books without dustjackets, with occasional exceptions
• Books that are so large or heavy that shipping them will cost you more than you are likely to make on the sale

And, generally speaking, any book that is extremely common for any reason so that its sellers have already glutted the market with copies for sale on the cheap

---

quarter each, and as one might expect they have been in unusually good condition for library discards. Perhaps because my competitors tend to shy away from library discards, there is seldom much price competition among these titles, and they usually bring somewhere over $10 each although I have a policy of never charging more than half the list price for these books. It is important to be especially fastidious in cataloguing and listing these books, or any books that turn up a "large print" description with their ISBN search, because the people who need them are in no position to hassle with you if they think they are ordering a good, clean large-print copy and receive something else in its place.

• Library discards don't have much of a good reputation among booksellers, and are certainly without value in almost every case for collectors, but a well-preserved ex-library copy of an uncommon title can bring a decent price simply as a reading copy or library edition from a buyer who has been searching out that book for years. Note that this is an exception to the minimum condition standard of "Very Good" or better suggested elsewhere in this book. Ordinarily I will not rate a library discard above "Good," but I believe library discards are worth acquiring if they are uncommon titles and are — aside from the usual stamps, labels, and lack of appeal for collectors — in "very good" condition.

Modern First Editions

One special class of **uncommon** books is **Modern First Editions**. Even among authors whose work is common or hyper-common, such as Grisham, Ludlum, Parker, Clancy, etc., there is a brisk market for Modern First Editions in fine or near fine condition, intact with fine dustjackets and no marks. They are far from scarce, and I would advise against paying more than a dollar for them, but there is a combination of three factors that provides you with a pretty good chance of selling them for somewhere between $25 and $30 each in Amazon's Marketplace (at this writing):

• Best-selling authors have large numbers of serious fans who may have read some of the books in paperback on the beach or in an airplane, but who may want a nice first-edition collection of their favorite novelist's work and be willing to pay a premium to build their libraries;

- Despite the fact that it may violate Amazon's listing rules, many sellers list unsigned Modern First Editions as "collectible", with the result that they cannot be priced below the list price for the title in question. Thus, if you are listing a fine first edition copy of John Grisham's *The Partner* as a collectible, you cannot set a price below $26.96. At this writing there are 19 "collectible" copies listed at this $26.96 price, and 17 of the 19 are described as first editions. Why add another to the mix? Well, they do sell at these prices, steadily if not briskly. And, it is important to know, Amazon's current practice is to display such listings, at each price point, on a "last listed, first displayed" basis, so if you list a copy with those 20 others today, yours will be the first a buyer sees, at least until the next one is listed by a seller, or, more happily, until your copy sells.

- There are also over 50 listed first edition copies of *The Partner* in "like new" or "very good" condition among the 324 hardcover copies classified not as "collectible" but as "used" by their sellers on Amazon's Marketplace. These first edition copies currently range in price between $2.25 and $18.85. Our anecdotal evidence tells us that, despite market forces related to lower prices, these copies have no better chance of selling for a lower price as a "used" copy, because the potential buyer has to slog through hundreds of listings to find them, than they do when listed at a higher price under the "collectible" classification.

The sheer numbers of first editions available when an author gets the kind of first-run printings that Grisham does obviously suggests that I've misclassified some of these books in my own classification system by calling them "uncommon." But I'll keep them here for now just because, functionally, if listed as prominently and strategically as you can list them, I believe that you can price and sell these books as if they were uncommon.

Identifying First Editions

Listing and selling a book as a first edition may bring a significantly higher price for the book, but it requires that the book be an actual first edition/first print copy, usually in near fine or better condition. Naturally, the first place to look is the copyright page inside, to see if "First Edition" is stated on that page. Once a book passes that test, the next steps are steps of elimination:

• Make sure that it is not a book club edition (BCE) by applying the BCE tests enumerated later in this chapter; many BCEs incorrectly state that they are first editions.

• Look for any dates on the copyright page that are later than the first edition publication date, since such dates would obviously eliminate the possibility that the book in your hands is a first edition.

• Satisfy yourself that the book is not a "reprinted first edition" published by a reprint publisher. The following are well-known reprint publishers: A.L. Burt, Altermus, Avenel, Blakiston, Cassel, Collier, Greenwich House, Cupples & Leon, Fiction Library, Goldsmith, Grosset & Dunlap, Hurst, Saalfield, Sun Dial, Tower, and Triangle.

• Look for a row of numbers on the copyright page that looks like one of these rows:

1 3 5 7 9 10 8 6 4 2

or

1 2 3 4 5 6 7 8 9 10

or

10 9 8 7 6 5 4 3 2 1

Publishers use these numerical strings to denote the printing (first, second, third, etc.) of a given edition that is represented. An intact string ordinarily means that a copy represents the first printing, and some publishers such as Random House let the words "First Edition" stand in place of the 1 and then use numerical strings whose lowest number is a 2. (Occasionally in place of a numerical string you will find an alphabetic string such as A B C D E, and the same rules apply). However, it is also necessary to be aware of the same problem of publisher sloppiness that sometimes plagues the administration of ISBNs: publishers often eave such details to the whim of employees at the low end of the pecking order and the followthrough can leave much to be desired. Consequently, the only thing that the numerical string can really prove to you is that, any time you see a lowest number of 3 or more in the numerical string, you can be sure that the book is not a first printing.

Once a book has passed these conventional tests, and is in fine or near fine condition, you may well have a collectible first edition, but if you stop here you always run the risk of having a buyer come back to you with the complaint that while the copy may be a "stated first edition," it is not a "true first edition/first print" copy. If you are not willing to spend the additional time to research an apparent first edition's "points" (a point, in this terminology, is a difference between one edition of a book and the next), I recommend that you do two things:

• List the book as a "stated first edition" rather than as a "first edition;" and

• Guarantee all items, which means that you will allow a no-hassle return and provide a full refund if a book is not what you thought it was.

But if you want to focus on modern first editions, it is well worth your time to keep working. To continue your investigation, we recommend that you explore the publisher-by-publisher information provided online in Glenn Larson's Guide to First Edition Identification on the website of the International Book Collector's Association at www.rarebooks.org/firsted.htm and consider acquiring and making use of some of the books suggested by my colleague Genevieve Kazdin in Appendix 3. Although some of its suggestions about specific books is dated, I strongly recommend Ian Ellis' ***Book Finds: How to Find, Buy and Sell Used and Rare Books*** as a good beginning point for the bookseller who wants to venture into the fields of modern first editions and scarce, rare, and antiquarian books. As you proceed, you will no doubt increase your knowledge base so that you will not need to go back to the research texts every time, and what will initially be time-consuming will eventually, in many cases, become second nature.

Scarce and Rare Books

With the rapid development of the Internet as a transparent global marketplace for books, the definitions of what books are scarce or rare have changed. Scarce books usually have significant value because they have a limited supply that is outstripped by the demand for them, but there are almost always some copies available for sale online, and you should be able to get some sense of the price market for such books by surveying the price and condition of these copies at used.addall.com. Some items are scarce for the simple, structural reason that there were physical limitations placed on the number originally "produced," such as limited edition printings and signed first editions. Truly rare books, on the other hand, are items that might come along once every few years, and you may not find a great deal of price guidance on the internet. Most general stock used booksellers will come across scarce and even rare books from time to time in the normal course of their acquisition process, and one's chances of making such finds will be improved the more one looks for uncommon books in the first place, and the more one learns and gains a feel for what kinds of books might be likely to be less common. But you'll also make great finds in commonplace haunts like library sales and thrift shops.

It would be futile to attempt to do justice to such a subject in a single chapter here, when there are shelves and shelves of very good books on the subject. The best I can do is to offer some guidance about where to pursue the kind of informal education that is a prerequisite for a seller who wishes to venture into the areas of scarce, rare, and antiquarian books, and perhaps to provide come encouragement as to why such a venture might be a worthwhile pursuit. There is a tremendous wealth of information available online, and I recommend beginning with the websites of the International Book Collectors Association (www.rarebooks.org) and the Antiquarian Booksellers' Association of America (www.abaa.org). When it comes to books on book collecting, I suggest you consult the excellent casual bibliography that my esteemed colleague Genevieve Kazdin (www.amazon.com/shops/dunesstudio) has provided for this project in Appendix 3. If you can find a bookseller with experience in these fields who is willing to let you serve a brief apprenticeship, you will be very lucky and should make every effort to take advantage.

The point made a few paragraphs ago about Amazon's "last in, first displayed" policy is an enormously important one, and it underlines the importance of regularly refreshing one's listings, an important marketing tactic that is addressed elsewhere in this book. We can probably file this one under "Do what I say and not what I do," but it is clear to me that, on average, smart booksellers go through 25 or more of their oldest listings each day in a systematic way to review whether they are still priced competitively and displayed prominently. This does not always mean lowering prices to stay competitive; I have often relisted titles with higher prices based on such a review. And I have also often found titles that were listed and priced as I wanted them, but which I took down and posted again in order to improve their placement in a list of several competitors' copies at the same price point.

It is possible that there are ethical issues that a seller should sort out in dealing with issues such as Amazon's instruction that **"You may select 'Collectible'" if your item is signed, out-of-print, or otherwise rare."** I have heard sellers justify their "collectible" classification, for example" of an unsigned copy of **The Partner** by saying that, by definition, a first-printing first edition is out of print as soon as the second printing gets underway. Although there is something about this rationale that makes me think a certain former saxophone-playing U.S. President's riff on the definition of "is" while being questioned about his Oval Office dalliances, I am nonetheless impressed with the creative thinking employed by these sellers, and I do not disagree with them. If Amazon believes that listing an unsigned first edition as "collectible" is a violation of its listing policies, I have certainly not seen any sign of that in terms of delisting or other sanctions. It is worth noting that the "collectible" classification practice increases Amazon's per-transaction profit, and it also is plausible that it improves the "customer experience" for those buyers who want to be able to find fine first editions easily, even though it means that they may pay a higher price for them than if they rooted around a while among the "used" listings.

Research: Tuning In to the Market

It is dangerous to attempt any advice about what books to acquire, because contemporary or "general stock" used book markets can change so quickly that they will make a fool of the advice-giver, so the best I can do here is to suggest first that if you are trying to make a living selling used general stock you should do regular and systematic research into demand, price market, and availability. The Internet makes it possible to do this very easily, using many of the same websites that we discuss elsewhere in this book as places to sell, and to a somewhat lesser extent as places to buy. In addition to the actual e-commerce sites where one could complete transactions directly, it also makes sense to pay attention to title-searching sites such as Used.addall.com and Bookfinder (www.bookfinder.com). Comb through these sites searching for titles, browsing subject areas, identifying the pricing and used-copy availability trends of current and recent best-sellers as well as strong backlist titles. Look for trends that will help you determine what items you might best take to Half.com as opposed to Amazon, and what would do better in an auction setting on eBay. None of us has time to be totally thorough about this kind of research, but an hour or two a week will pay off significantly in your ongoing efforts to find the best markets for your listings. Here are some suggestions about places to conduct your research:

- www.amazon.com, with attention to subject best seller lists, Marketplace searches sorted by price, author searches, and special lists such as previous year bestsellers and award-winners

- www.half.com, using the relatively new category-searching functions to browse category best-sellers and note pricing trends

- www.ebay.com, by clicking on "Browse" and exploring successful auctions

- Used.addall.com's tag line invites you to "search, compare, and save at 40 bookstores, 20,000 dealers, and millions of books." It won't search Amazon or eBay for you, but it will give you a fairly speedy search of every used copy of any title you enter that is available from, at this writing, Advanced Book Exchange, Alibris, Antiqbook, Bibliology, Biblion, Bibliopoly, Biblioroom, Elephantbooks, Half.com, ILAB, JustBooks.co.uk, and Powell's Books, with full listing information. Now if that doesn't give you some sense of the market for a book, then one of two things is true. Either we're talking about a very scarce book for which you are likely to make a lot of money, or a very dense bookseller who is not likely to make much money at all.

One way of tuning into your market is to develop areas of specialization, since one individual cannot possibly become expert in all areas of the used book market simultaneously. Start with what you know and love and hone that knowledge until it becomes real and marketable expertise, whether the field is literary fiction, poetry, mysteries, travel books, cookbooks, computer books, business books, military history, baseball, religion, large-print books, illustrated books – well, you catch my drift – it really can be any area you desire to expand your familiarity with.

Identifying Book Club Editions

Book Club Editions (BCEs) have little or no value for book collectors and should in most cases be avoided. The mere fact that a book club edition has been printed suggests that a title is common and, therefore, unlikely to fetch a very good price, either, from the market of non-collecting readers. The trick, then, is to educate oneself to recognize and avoid the telltale signs that a particular copy may indeed be a book club edition. Here are some common signs:

• Many BCEs include the printed words "Book Club Edition" at the bottom of the inside flap of the front cover.

• A hardcover, dustjacketed book without a price at the top of the inside flap of the front cover is usually, but not always, a BCE. (The most common exceptions to this "rule" come from university, academic, and small independent presses, which sometimes avoid printing the price so permanently on their books, largely because a small print run may last for several years and necessarily undergo pricing changes due to market changes).

- A book which has experienced the clipping or cutting of either the bottom of the inside flap of the front cover, or both the bottom and the top of the inside flap of the front cover, is very likely to be a BCE.

- If you have other reasons to suspect a book is a BCE, such as inferior paper quality or smaller size, don't be thrown off the scent by a clipped "price corner." It may well be that what was clipped was not the price, but the absence of a price, in an effort to disguise a BCE.

- However, printed words such as "A Selection of the Book-of-the-Month Club" or "A Main Selection of the Literary Guild" do not mean that a copy is a BCE; indeed, they probably mean the opposite. Publishers print these phrases on trade editions of their books for their marketing power, in order to signal to prospective bookstore buyers the popularity of the titles in question.

- Any other reference to BOMC, the Book-of-the-Month Club, or any other book club on the copyright page or anywhere else on a book strongly indicates that a copy is a BCE copy.

- BCEs often state on the copyright page that they are First Editions. Of course, they are not.

- BCEs often have a depression such as a circle, dot, square, maple leaf, or similar mark, sometimes in red, on the bottom of the back cover.

- Recent BCEs often have a rectangular block on the lower right back dustcover with an adjacent four- or five-digit number.

- Although the vast majority of BCEs are reprints of trade hardcovers, there are several books that are the first hardcover editions of paperback originals and a very few that are indeed true first editions. In some but not all cases these BCEs may have value not usually associated with BCEs.

VII   Where To Sell Your Books

The Internet provides a wide array of selling venue choices for the prospective online bookseller, but it is possible to waste a great deal of time and effort trying to diversify one's listings when there may not be any good business reason for doing so. From a business point of view, it is important to begin by making a list of the factors that might be important to you in determining where to list your books. Here are my suggestions:

- What sites offer the most traffic?
- Within that traffic volume, how many visitors come to the site with their credit cards ready for the express purpose of buying books?
- Within a site, how prominently and strategically will your listings be displayed?
- What are the user-friendliness issues involved in a particular selling venue, both for your prospective buyers and for you as a seller?
- What are the costs of listing and selling your books on a particular venue?
- How much of your catalogue can you list prominently on a given venue?

Rather than try to adopt a false guise of impartiality, let me say that I have studied these questions long and hard and concluded long ago that the Amazon Marketplace is overwhelmingly the most profitable place to sell books online, *provided that the books one is attempting to list are in the Amazon catalogue*. Here's my take:

- Other sites such as search engines or information sites may rival Amazon in traffic, but they are not primarily e-commerce sites.

- Amazon is the world's largest Internet retailer, and more people come to Amazon to purchase books than all other Internet retailers and databases combined.

- The Amazon Marketplace (as opposed to zShops or Amazon Auctions) allows the highest profile of display prominence for third-party book listings of any site on the Internet, and the results of this strategic prominence are borne out by the fact that over 23% of all transactions involve third-party sellers, as of the first quarter of 2002.

- Amazon is absolutely top-shelf when it comes to user-friendliness for its ultimate customers.

- Amazon's user-friendliness for sellers leaves much to be desired, with frequent glitches that can prove frustrating or worrisome for sellers. These frustrations and the fact that Amazon offers its Marketplace, zShop, and Auction services on an "as is" basis notwithstanding, Amazon is still at least as good as, and possibly superior to its competitors when it comes to ease of use for sellers.

- The cost of doing business on Amazon is amazingly low when one thinks of it as "rent" for prime selling space in the world's largest e-commerce mall: an Amazon Pro Merchant account is $39.99 per month, and a seller then pays what is effectively a commission of 15 per cent of the selling price of each sold item. (The Pro Merchant account is an option, and you also have the choice of not paying it and instead paying an additional 99 cents per unit for each sold item, but this only makes sense for the casual or very low-volume seller. If you have spent the money to buy this book, I would recommend that, once you have gone through a brief experimental period, you try to get to the point as soon as possible where you can spend the money to become a Pro Merchant seller and take the steps necessary to make sure that you sell the 40 items per month necessary to eat up that $39.99).

- Aside from politics, the primary factor that drives sellers to venues other than Amazon is the lack of a universal catalogue, something that Amazon claims to be working on. Currently sellers of most pre-ISBN books (that is, books more than about 30 years old) cannot sell them on the Amazon Marketplace. If, however, you are dealing with a general stock of more or less contemporary used books, Amazon will allow you to list prominently the vast majority of books you acquire.

If Amazon is the easiest and most cost-effective venue for listing general stock books online, then Half.com runs a strong, if not close, second. If you are just starting out as an online seller of general stock, you will probably want to limit your initial activity to these two venues. If you also carry some collectible or older items that you are unable to list on Amazon or Half.com, or interesting groups of books that might best be sold as "lots," you may also want to consider eBay as an initial venue.

Once you begin contemplating more than a single venue for selling, it is time to consider two extremely important and related issues:

- *The sticky problem of "out of stock" updating.* If you are going to list the same copies simultaneously on multiple venues, you will need to establish, on the front end, an air-tight system for updating your listings on all affected sites to reflect and take out of inventory your sold copies. Some multiple-venue sellers avoid duplicating their listings from site to site because they are not confident in their solutions to these problems, and even the most well-organized system or software can be sabotaged by a fiasco such as a period of roughly two weeks in the Spring of 2002 when Amazon's site maintenance problems made it impossible for many sellers to update or edit existing listings.

- Any well-organized solution to the challenge of updating sold listings in multiple venues will necessarily involve the use of a database, and a good starting point for considering such software is to take a look at a service called BookRouter (www.bookrouter.com) that, for a fee, will handle all of your uploading, price adjustments, deletions, and other processing for as many selling venues as you wish to deal with. BookRouter charges a setup fee of $50 and a monthly fee of $25 for up to five sites, with an additional $5 on each fee for each additional site. BookRouter will work with virtually any software configuration a seller might use. I recommend that you begin this exploration by reading BookRouter's Glossary and Primer at bookrouter.com/brglossary.html.

In any case, as you gain experience and perhaps develop a range of listings that goes beyond general stock, you may well want to branch out for any number of reasons, including selling advantages, your desire to support bookseller databases, and your perception that it would be wise not to keep all your eggs in a single basket. Here is a list, with basic contact information, of bookselling venues you may wish to explore:

Amazon Marketplace

URL: www.amazon.com/marketplace

EMAIL: sellers-support@amazon.com

TELEPHONE: 800-201-7575 or 877-251-0696 (Between 6 a.m. and 7 p.m. Pacific time, Monday through Friday)

FAX: 206-266-2950

FEE STRUCTURE: Amazon uses a two-tiered fee structure for third party sellers. If you anticipate selling 10 items a week or more, you will want to become a Pro Merchant Seller so that you can list an unlimited number of items, waive the 99-cent-per-item transaction fee, and pay only Amazon's 15 per cent commission (this includes credit card processing). The Pro Merchant fee is $39.99 per month and will be listed in your Amazon.com Payments account summary and charged against existing account funds. In the event of a negative account balance, the Seller's registered credit card will be charged for outstanding fees.

DESCRIPTION: Individuals and businesses can buy and sell used and collectible books, music, DVDs, videos, console-based video games, electronics items, tools, and photography equipment directly on the product information page where Amazon.com sells the same item new, provided that the item to be listed is already in Amazon's catalogue. "There is no finer real estate online," claims Amazon, and it is hard to argue with the claim given Amazon's customer base of roughly 30 million. All payments are always processed online by Amazon Payments and will clear into your account in about five days, or biweekly if you do not initiate the transfers yourself.

Amazon zShops and Auctions
URL: www.amazon.com/zshops

EMAIL: seller-support@amazon.com; community-help@amazon.com - report a community rules violation; reports@amazon.com - report abuse

TELEPHONE: 800-201-7575 or 877-251-0696 (Between 6 a.m. and 7 p.m. Pacific time, Monday through Friday)

FAX: 206-266-2950

FEE STRUCTURE: zShops listing fees of 10 cents per item and transaction fees of 5% for the first $25 and 2.5% above $25. Payment processing fees for payments made through Amazon Payments are $0.25 per item, plus 2.5% of the transaction amount, but Sellers may also accept other forms of payment. Per-item listing fees are waived for Pro Merchant sellers, whose subscription fee of $39.99 per month is listed in their Amazon.com Payments account summary and charged against any sales they have completed.

DESCRIPTION: Fixed-price and auction options for items not listed in the Amazon catalogue, with zShops storefronts and access – but far less site prominence than Amazon Marketplace – to Amazon's customer base. You may list "almost anything under the sun" for sale and cross-link it to Amazon items to attract buyers, but the cross-links (which used to be quite prominent before the advent of Amazon Marketplace) can be almost impossible to find, because they often require a buyer to scroll down a half-dozen or more screens. It will be interesting to see if Amazon finds an effective way to re-tool and improve the prominence of zShops; at this writing many long-time zShops-only sellers express a feeling of abandonment by Amazon since the advent of Marketplace.

Half.com
URL: www.half.ebay.com/products/books/index.cfm

EMAIL: books@half.com or Info@half.com

TELEPHONE: (888) 879-4253 or 1 (800) 545-9857

FEE STRUCTURE: "At Half.com, there are no start-up, listing or monthly fees. We simply take a commission off the selling price at the time of the sale." The commission structure begins at 15% for items under $50, 12.5% between $50 and $100, 10% between $100 and $250, etc.

DESCRIPTION: Initially established by Josh Kopelman as a fixed-price marketplace for used books in July 1999, Half.com was acquired by eBay one year later and now allows sellers to offer new or used books, music, and video products. Half.com has attracted a high volume of sellers and buyers, although far fewer than Amazon Marketplace, and offers over 50 million items for sale. The imbalance between sellers and buyers is evident in the fact that Half.com has price markets considerably lower than those on Amazon Marketplace, even with a 75-cent price minimum, on the vast majority of items except those where the Marketplace price is below 75 cents. Otherwise, Half.com is extremely user-friendly and tends to create a smooth listing and selling experience.

EBay Auctions

URL: www.ebay.com

EMAIL: eBay discourages direct email contact by does provide a web-based email support system at www.pages.ebay.com/help/basics/select-support.html

FEE STRUCTURE: eBay charges a listing fee of between $.30 and $3.30 depending on the minimum bid set by a seller, a final value fee that ranges from 1.50% to 5.25% of the final sale price, and an eBay Payments fee of $.35 plus 3% for transactions over $15 or a flat $.35 for transactions under $15.

DESCRIPTION: eBay is the world's largest internet auction site and hosts millions of book transactions each year. Its high traffic makes it a good place to sell books that are not in the Amazon catalogue, particularly those that are relatively scarce. Many sellers also have had success selling "lots" of books in particular interest categories such as older mysteries, sports books, etc., on eBay. Learning the ropes of auction-selling is a must for those who hope to do significant business on eBay, and we recommend a series of articles by auction bookseller Craig Stark that are available at *AuctionBytes*, beginning at this web address: http://www.auctionbytes.com/cab/abu/y201/m06/abu0039/s05

Advanced Book Exchange

URL: www.abebooks.com

EMAIL: ABE Financial: invoice@abebooks.com; ABE/Half.com Program: half.com@abebooks.com; Web-based "Help Wizard" at www.dogbert.abebooks.com/abe/ActionRequestInsert

TELEPHONE: 1-800-315-5335 6AM-10PM Mon-Fri; 10AM-2PM Sat PST

FAX: 1 - 250 - 475 - 6016

FEE STRUCTURE: Instead of collecting from booksellers when a book is sold, Abebooks charges an up-front monthly subscription rate based on the number of titles listed. At this writing, the monthly fee for U.S. booksellers is $25 for up to 500 titles, $37 for 501 to 4,000 titles, $42 to 4,001 to 10,000 titles, and $53 for 10,001 to 20,000 titles.

DESCRIPTION: Abebooks, a network of about 9,000 independent booksellers, is a private company, registered in Victoria, B.C., Canada. Founded by Keith Waters and Rick Pura, it launched in 1996 and provides its members with the online capability of selling their books to customers worldwide. In the Fall of 2001, ABEBooks acquired European JustBooks, enabling further expansion into the international marketplace. Abebooks has over 35 million rare, antiquarian, used and out-of-print book listings, and to the extent possible within the Half.com catalogue, its listings are also listed on Half.com, just as at this writing Alibris' listings are also listed on Amazon Marketplace. Abebooks provides a free database software program called Homebase, specifically designed with used, rare, and out-of-print booksellers in mind, which is free and downloadable from the Abebooks website at www.abebooks.com. "By combining the inventories of our member booksellers into a common database and coupling it with advanced search capabilities, e-commerce facilities, and partnership programs, ABEBooks has become a dominant player in the Internet book market," says the Abebooks website.

Alibris

URL: www.alibris.com

EMAIL: sellers@alibris.com

SNAIL MAIL: Alibris, 1250 45th Street, Suite 100 Emeryville, CA 94608.

FEE STRUCTURE: Alibris takes a 20% commission from the price paid by the ultimate customers and sends the balance to the seller. Alibris has historically provided sellers with prepaid shipping labels so that they can send ordered books to Alibris at no cost beyond the cost of packaging.

DESCRIPTION: Alibris is both a bookseller in its own right, with its own in-house inventory, and a centralized listings service, with centralized shipping and ordering for its member sellers. Alibris in turn lists many of its members' books on Amazon Marketplace, which has raised concerns about redundancy for some sellers. Alibris' "partners," the sellers who list their books with Alibris, have historically shipped sold items directly to Alibris which repackages them and sends them on to the ultimate customers, but at this writing Alibris appears to be changing this approach.

Antiqbook

URL: www.antiqbook.com

EMAIL: nan@antiqbook.nl

FEE STRUCTURE: Rather than hazard an effort to translate the Euro into U.S. currency, let us say here that the fee structure is organized in a fashion similar to ABEBooks', but is slightly lower.

DESCRIPTION: An independent book listing service of the Netherlands Antiquarian Booksellers' Network, based out of the Netherlands

BiblioDirect.com

URL: www.BiblioDirect.com

EMAIL: admin@BiblioDirect.com . "If you have a question, just log onto www.BiblioDirect.com and click on the icon in the upper right hand corner. If there is an operator on-line, you may ask the question and get an immediate response; if we're offline at the moment, it will direct you to an e-mail address. If you have any questions, suggestions or issues, or need dealer/buyer conflict resolution please send them to: jan@BiblioDirect.com"

FEE STRUCTURE: Instead of collecting from booksellers when a book is sold, BiblioDirect charges an up-front monthly subscription rate based on the number of titles listed. At this writing, the monthly fee for U.S. booksellers is $25 for up to 1,000 titles, $30 for 1,001 to 4,999 titles, $35 to 5,000 to 9,999 titles, and $40 for 10,000 to 19,999 titles.

DESCRIPTION: "Biblio*Direct*.com (incorporated as Bibliophile Books, Inc.) was conceived by three booksellers: Lynn DeWeese-Parkinson, who has a store by that name in Forest Grove, Oregon, and Roger and Jan O'Connor, who own Mostly Books in Pittsburg, Kansas. As long-time booksellers themselves (more than 100 years of collective experience), they wanted to bring back the traditional standards, values, practices, and competence of the book trade to the innovative world of Internet bookselling. Biblio*Direct*.com is designed to facilitate the transaction between the buyer and the seller without getting in the middle. All transactions are made at the dealer's price and under the dealer's terms with no mark-ups, additional shipping fees, or commissions."

Bibliology

URL: www.bibliology.com

EMAIL:membership@bibliology.com   or enquries@bibliology.com

FEE STRUCTURE: "Books are listed on the basis of a monthly subscription, with the benefit of a secure ordering system. There are no further charges or commissions." The monthly fee is 25 pounds for up to 5,000 listings, 35 pounds for 5,001 to 10,000 listings, 40 pounds for 10,001 to 20,000 listings, and so forth.

DESCRIPTION: "The on-line book fair", UK-based Bibliogy, describes itself as "a secure and informative book site, with an excellent search mechanism, where booksellers and book buyers come together…. Bibliology does not interfere in the relationship between booksellers and their customers."

Biblion

URL: www.biblion.com

EMAIL: www.biblion.com/contact.php

TELEPHONE: 020 7495 0219, between 9am and 6pm GMT Monday to Friday.

FEE STRUCTURE: For listings of 1,000 books or more, a monthly fee of 29.37 pounds (this includes the British Value Added Tax, or sales tax, of 17.5%). If prepaid annually, there is a discount equal to two months' fees. Or, as a third option, sellers may forego the subscription fee altogether and instead pay a commission of 11.75% (this commission also includes the Value Added Tax).

DESCRIPTION: A UK-based antiquarian and rare book listings service.

Bibliophile

URL: www.bibliophile.net

EMAIL: benson@bibliophile.net

TELEPHONE: +41 1 364 57 11

FEE STRUCTURE: "Bibliophile.net is currently a free listing service. If and when we charge a listing fee, it will be based on the number of books listed."

DESCRIPTION: "We are a privately-held, independent company and intend to stay that way," says Jack Benson of Swiss-based Bibliophile. "Our listing service has been on-line for three years in its present format. We are the first to admit that sales are still low compared to those generated by our bigger competitors, in large part due to limitations in what we can spend on advertising. This is the price of independence. Nevertheless, we sell several hundred books per week for our booksellers, and these numbers are rising steadily. Our multilingual interface targets additional markets for your books."

BookAvenue

URL: www.bookavenue.co

EMAIL: info@bookavenue.com

FEE STRUCTURE: Instead of collecting from booksellers when a book is sold, BookAvenue charges an up-front monthly subscription rate based on the number of titles listed. At this writing, the monthly fee for U.S. booksellers is $9.95 for up to 1,999 titles, $19.95 for 2,000 to 24,999 titles, etc.

DESCRIPTION: A centralized listing service that describes its transactions as follows: "When your books(s) are matched with customers search criteria, your dealer information will be displayed along with the below text as your terms of sale. You may want to include such things as additional costs to the customer, return information, what types of payment you accept, etc."

Books & Collectibles

URL: www.booksandcollectibles.com.au

EMAIL: admin@booksandcollectibles.com.au

FEE STRUCTURE: Instead of collecting from booksellers when a book is sold, Books and Collectibles charges an up-front monthly subscription rate based on the number of titles listed. At this writing, the monthly fee is $25 Australian for up to 1,999 titles, $40 Australian for 2,000 to 10,000 titles, $50 Australian for 10,001 to 40,000 titles, etc. As an introductory offer, the first two months of service are free.

DESCRIPTION: Books and Collectibles is an Australian listings service for antiquarian, rare, out of print and new books, plus antiques, fine arts and collectibles. All transactions are between buyer and seller; Books and Collectibles acts as a meeting point between parties.

TomFolio

URL: www.tomfolio.com

EMAIL: www.tomfolio.com/sendmessage.asp?type=2

SNAIL MAIL: TomFolio, P.O. Box 392, Readville, MA 02137

FEE STRUCTURE: Instead of collecting from booksellers when a book is sold, TomFolio charges an up-front monthly listing fee ($35 for up to 4,000 titles, $40 for 4,001 to 10,000 titles, $45 for

10,001 to 25,000 titles, etc.) based on the number of titles listed. Members are also encouraged to become co-operative share owners for $500, payable either in a lump sum or in 10 monthly payments.

DESCRIPTION: A bookseller-owned listings service, run by the ABookCoop independent booksellers cooperative.

Getting Rid of Your Deadwood

Once you have determined that you cannot sell a given book online at a price that makes it worthwhile, you don't necessarily have to give up on it, assuming it is good enough shape to pass it on. It makes good sense for an online seller to develop and cultivate some offline selling venues short of the ponderously expensive project of actually opening up a brick-and-mortar bookstore, and here are a few to consider:

• You may well be able to sell your unwanted books to existing brick-and-mortar *used bookshops*, either for cash or, better yet, for a higher trading credit with which you can pick over bargain items in their inventory for which you believe you will be able to find an online buyer. This kind of trading obviously requires an instinct or feel for the books you are acquiring that will likely grow much better with experience, so don't get in over your head before you know what you are doing.

• *Yard sales, garage sales, flea markets,* and *antique malls* are great places to unload unwanted book inventory for small amounts of cash, and you don't necessarily have to be the one holding the sale or renting the space. Keep an eye out for the friend, neighbor, or relative who is planning such a sale or who rents space at a flea market or antique mall and see if you can make a deal at 50-50 or better.

• My favorite option, partly because it is easy, final, and does not depend on the whim of a buyer, is to *donate such inventory back to the local public library*. Yes, I am in business to make money, but I also endeavor to be a good citizen. Besides that, it does make money by giving one a deduction at tax time based on the amount you paid for each book, and it also helps create good will at the library, which is as important a place to have good will as any, given the fact that it is a major source of used books. And I have never had one of the librarians diss one of my discards by saying, "Uh, no, I don't think we'd be interested in that!"

VIII   Grading And Describing Your Books

As Amazon says on its website, "An honest appraisal of the used and collectible items listed for sale at Amazon Marketplace is the first step toward ensuring a great experience for both buyer and seller." Toward that end, it is incumbent upon every seller who wants to be successful to take pains to grade and describe their books accurately and consistently, to inspect each book carefully in a well-lit environment so that you don't miss and/or fail to disclose its flaws, and to avoid the silly trap of trying to improve a five-dollar book's sales potential by glossing over a flaw whose non-disclosure will upset a buyer sufficiently to leave you damning "customer feedback" that will cost you a lot more than five dollars in sales.

One of the challenges that we face with the explosion of the online used book market is that it is likely to attract a growing number of customers who lack familiarity with the jargon, abbreviations, and terminology employed by used and antiquarian booksellers to describe their wares. While the phrase "good reading copy" may communicate to an experienced buyer that he is buying a book whose only value is that it will survive fairly well through a few more readings, many of us have learned the hard way it is no longer sufficient to rely on that phrase to describe the book to the uninitiated:

"What do you mean – 'Good reading copy?' There was a name and phone number inside, and three pages were dog-eared, and there was highlighting and underlining in Chapter Twelve!"

I trust that you catch my drift. You don't (I hope) want to be the kind of biblio-snob who slams his potential customers for not knowing the difference between a "good reading copy" and an "advance reading copy," but on the other hand you need to have a clear sense of the terminology that your customers are equipped to understand so that you can use that terminology to communicate with them and market to them rather than to eliminate them

In any case the beginning point for any used bookseller must be to familiarize himself with the terminology of the trade, including the gradings and definitions shown in the box on page 104, the Book Collector's Glossary in Appendix 1, and the various abbreviations and descriptive phrases shown throughout this chapter. The glossary is especially helpful in learning the trade's names for the parts of a book, whether or not you decide to fill your descriptions for your customers with references to "boards," "leaves," and similar terms.

Booksellers have worked long and hard to codify a simple and straightforward set of gradings for used and antiquarian books, and for the most part they have tended to be fairly consistent with one another. Let's start here at the most simple, straightforward level, with a table on the next page that shows the gradings stated by Amazon on its own Marketplace site, since these are the gradings and definitions most often seen by online used book buyers. These gradings and definitions are quite strict and clear and you will only be setting yourself up for a fall if you over-ride them. Several things are especially worthy of note about these gradings and definitions:

- Many new books that you can find on the shelves of a new book physical bookstore are not up to the "perfect condition" standard cited by Amazon, and generally accepted in other grading systems, for "new" books and "like new" used books. Some online booksellers use this discrepancy as an excuse for unilaterally lowering the standards so that they apply to their books, but they do so at some risk to their own business reputation and to the overall customer experience in the online book market.

- Amazon's definitions imply, without clearly stating it, that a hardcover book lacking its original dustcover should never be listed as "Good" or better. This is not consistent with other grading systems that we have seen, and is apparently a result of Amazon's arbitrary concatenation of gradings for book and dustcover, which used and antiquarian booksellers have traditionally separated in gradings such as "VG/G." If you are going to over-ride this definition, the risk is as described in the previous paragraph, and the responsibility is clearly yours to state as boldly as possible that the otherwise "good" or better book lacks a dustcover.

• Amazon's "Unacceptable" grading makes a clear policy statement that uncorrected proofs, advance reading copies, and "books that are distributed for promotional use only" must not be sold on Amazon's Marketplace. "Books that are distributed for promotional use only" means review copies, unless I am missing something, and goes to the heart of an age-old debate for used booksellers. There have been some large and prominent used bookstores in Manhattan that would not have existed if it were not for their ability to acquire review copies, but publishers have generally claimed that they should be able to control, from on high, the secondary markets of their review copies and have occasionally gone to great lengths to "persuade" booksellers not to traffic in such forbidden fruit. These publishers would have reviewers destroy review copies once they are through with them, which often is the day they arrive in the mail. Used booksellers have countered with claims that it is the book-buying public that pays for the production of review copies in the first place and should have the opportunity to buy them again at retail, somewhat more cheaply, and that a book is, let's put this prettily, a kind of "living thing" whose life should not be snuffed out because of the economic claims of a greedy publishing industry. In any case, at this writing there are thousands of advanced reading copies for sale not only at Amazon, but in virtually every brick and mortar used bookshop in the United States, so the efforts of publishers to control the market that they created in the first place have been utterly futile.

But we digress.

Let's be clear here about the fact that Amazon is not the only source or the definitive source on the definitions of these book condition gradings. We have decided to lead with them as a simple gesture of deference to reality, because it is clear that more book buyers and booksellers will come into contact with Amazon's grading definitions than with any other set of definitions this year and for years to come. We're going to be selling some books in Rome, so let's make sure we know what the Romans are doing.

If you would like to compare the Amazon definitions with some other sets of grading definitions, we suggest you visit **Bibliomania** (www.bibliomania.net/Lesson1.html) and the **Independent Online Booksellers Association** (www.ioba.org/desc.html).

Once you select the appropriate rating for a book, you'll want to post a description that adds other detailed information letting prospective buyers in on the rest of the story. There are several challenges; the first is to fit your description into the 70-character line that Amazon allows for regular used books posted manually. (Amazon allows a 200-character description for new and collectible books as well as any books loaded automatically, in bulk, through its Inventory Loader or Book Loader functions).

The ethics of providing accurate used book descriptions demands the disclosure of all flaws in a book you are listing, but the space limitations of Amazon's 70-character description field can make full disclosure a very challenging task. Half.com moved early in 2002 to expand the description field available to sellers, and one would hope that Amazon would move quickly to take the same step, one that would certainly be consistent with improving the overall customer experience.

In any case, your first job in making yourself a good describer of your books is to familiarize yourself with the terminology of the enterprise including the names given to a book's parts, the jargon used to describe common book flaws (such as "foxing", which is not an early Valley Girl expression for cruising the mall looking for dudes), and the common abbreviations. We suggest you familiarize yourself with the glossary and descriptive abbreviations found in the Appendices at the end of this book, and then try to come to your best judgment as to what balance you should strike between jargon and abbreviations on the one hand, and accessible common parlance on the other.

Some sellers believe they should never use abbreviations such as "dj" for dustjacket or "mm pbk" for mass market paperback. Call me a hopeless optimist, but my instinct here is to believe that buyers can figure out abbreviations when the word behind the abbreviation is not too obscure.

Some Tips on Writing Good Descriptions

- Don't claim that a book is first edition unless you can provide proof; if you aren't sure; you can always fall back on "possible 1st edition" or "stated 1st edition," for what they are worth.
- Don't ever overstate a book's condition or make claims you can't back up, or you will learn the hard way just how often such practices can come back to bite you
- A book that one might list as "rare" in a neighborhood bookstore may not be "rare" online, so beware of putting off knowledgeable customers by making such generalized claims
- There's nothing wrong with using a little graphic impact such as a few asterisks or an upper-case word to make a listing stand out from others, but don't become a carnival barker – this is bookselling, and we pretend to a certain level of decorum, even if you *are* posting books in your pajamas
- Avoid being subjective or describing a book in the context of its age, e.g., "pretty good for its age" or "well-preserved." Describe the book's condition, and give the publication date if that is applicable and not redundant, but don't get one mixed up with the other.
- If you have the space, don't be afraid to have a little fun with your descriptions. Our esteemed colleague Forrest Proper of Joslin Hall Rare Books passed along this description in the listing of a first edition of Jane Austen's Pride and Prejudice in the Biblioctopus Antiquarian Books catalog (www.biblioctopus.com): "the leather is smooth as caramel and the pages are whiter than Dad's legs". A little personality never hurt a retail enterprise. Well, almost never.

After all, we are talking here about people who are buying books, not athletic socks. But remember that obscure abbreviations and jargon may just confuse the buyer and lead to a bad transaction, so don't try to impress your potential buyer with terms he has never seen before.

You can save yourself valuable space by avoiding descriptive text (such as "mass market paperback") that is redundant with the material already provided by Amazon for the ISBN that you are using to post the book. While it is true that traditionally a bookseller's descriptions have been standardized to include Author, Title, Publisher, Publication City, Publication Date, Book Description, Price, Format, Edition, and Description of Condition, only the last two of these items needs to be in a Half.com or Amazon Marketplace book description; the others are probably redundant unless there is a marketing reason for including them.

Whether you are entering titles manually one at a time or using a bulk loading function such as Amazon's Book Loader, you will want to employ some shortcuts both to speed up a slow process and also to help you establish consistency in noting the important distinguishing characteristics about your books.

One useful trick involves the "Auto-Complete" function in recent versions of Internet Explorer. With this function, you may have noticed when filling out an online form that is you begin typing in your zip code, 0 ... 2 ..., it will complete the field and give you a choice of all the zip codes you have recently entered that begin with the digits 0 and 2. I also keep a Word file of my descriptive one-liners open when I am posting, so that I can easily cut and paste tried and true descriptions into the entry field if one of them applies to a book I have in front of me, ready to post online. (This kind of description recycling also takes the pain out of what can otherwise be one of the more nudgy and time-consuming elements of the posting process, which is trying to stay within the 70-character limit). I also suspect, without any scientific data to back me up, that is can be reassuring to potential buyers to see the same descriptive phrases again and again (assuming, of course, that they are accurate!) rather than having to figure out exactly what a seller means (or is trying to hide) with some new turn of phrase.

Of course, one of the best ways to strengthen your approach to writing good book descriptions is to see what some other top-notch sellers are doing in that regard, so let us direct you now to a few Amazon storefronts where once you arrive you can click on the link that says: "See all dunesstudio's zShop listings" to view the clear and concise book descriptions that have helped earn these sellers their five-star customer feedback ratings:

- Dunes Studio (www.amazon.com/shops/dunesstudio)

- JunebugBooks (www.amazon.com/shops/junebugbooks)

- Lcplbob (www.amazon.com/shops/lcplbob)

- Watafind Shoppe (www.amazon.com/shops/watafind)

- Meremc (www.amazon.com/shops/meremc)

Amazon Marketplace
Condition Guidelines: Books

New and used books must be listed at a price that is at or below the Amazon.com price. They may be sold at any price when the item is listed as out of stock or out of print by Amazon.com. **Collectible books** must be signed, out of print, or otherwise unique--you will have an opportunity to detail why your copy is collectible. Such books must be listed at a price that is greater than the list price.

- *New:* Just like it sounds. A brand-new, unused, unread copy in perfect condition.

- *Like New:* An apparently unread copy in perfect condition. Dust cover is intact; pages are clean and are not marred by notes or folds of any kind. Suitable for presenting as a gift.

- *Very Good:* A copy that has been read, but remains in excellent condition. Pages are intact and are not marred by notes or highlighting. The spine remains undamaged.

- *Good:* A copy that has been read, but remains in clean condition. All pages are intact, and the cover is intact (including dust cover, if applicable). The spine may show signs of wear. Pages can include limited notes and highlighting, and the copy can include "From the library of" labels.

- *Acceptable:* A readable copy. All pages are intact, and the cover is intact (the dust cover may be missing). Pages can include considerable notes--in pen or highlighter--but the notes cannot obscure the text.

- *Unacceptable:* Moldy, badly stained, or unclean copies are not acceptable, nor are copies with missing pages or obscured text. Books that are distributed for promotional use only are prohibited. This includes advance reading copies (ARCs) and uncorrected proof copies.

Some Bad Book Descriptions

Here, with absolutely no attribution to or permission from their very creative authors, are some book descriptions seen recently for Used Books listed at Amazon.com and Half.com. They should be embarrassing to the sellers in question, but much worse, they damage the overall Marketplace, particularly since many buyers don't pay sufficient attention to the descriptions when they buy the book in the first place.

- 1998 edition. Not this book, but it's still a book. Nice!
- Like new - name label on inside cover
- Like New - small scratches/ bent corners on cover, a few passages hi-lighted
- Collectible Like New - 1982 Holt Reinhart and Winston, HC, BCE, Dust Jacket shows edge wear, small half inch tear upper left
- New - NEW MANUFACTURERS OVERSTOCK FRONT COVER REMOVED
- Like New - Brand New, no dust cover, owners name on 1st page
- Like new- highlighting
- Acceptable: blood stains on front cover and some inside
- Good - is very good shape little creases on spine mint condition.
- Vg+ condition in vg+ dj. Light ex-Lib of Congress markings to opening pgs., rear hinge just barely separating

Full Disclosure: Book Flaws That Must Be Noted In A Good Seller's Book Description

- Book club edition or co-branded non-retail edition
- Library discard or "ex-library"
- Damp staining
- Binding flaws or weakness
- Tears
- Edge wear and chipping of dustjacket or boards
- Underlining, highlighting, notes, and marginalia
- Musty odor (never stock or sell such a book)
- Foxing (reddish brown discoloration of pages)
- Age toning
- Soiling of cover or pages
- Bookplates
- Previous owners' names, notes, and gift inscriptions
- Labels and stamps
- Any defect that has resulted in a grade of less than "Like New", although if these are barely visible you may sometimes group them with a phrase such as "slight reading wear"

IX   Posting And Pricing Your Books

The real value of any book is what an informed buyer will pay you for it, and this depends on its availability, its condition, and your access to the marketplace of buyers.

In this chapter we will walk through the nuts and bolts tasks of listing your books online. Maybe the next line here is just an author's ego speaking, but hey, I am well aware that this is not *Ulysses* or *The Brothers Karamazov* or even *Tourist Season*, so I don't think so: *Even if you have listed thousands of books online, it is probably worth your taking five minutes and reading through the following primer at least one time on the off chance you will pick up a valuable tidbit that will help you sell your books more profitably and more quickly in the future.* That's my story and I'm sticking to it.

If you are selling a book on Amazon's Marketplace or on Half.com, there's no need to take or scan pictures, or to worry about any HTML-related presentation issues. Your book will be presented quite seamlessly and prominently, unless there is a glut of copies. All you have to do to post the book is find the right edition by ISBN or title and small print, then determine your classification and condition rating and write a brief description of its condition. While we will address these processes first, we will also spend some time later in this chapter on the special importance of presentation if you are listing titles on eBay, Amazon zShops or Auctions, your own website, or any number of other sites mentioned elsewhere in this book.

.   (ISBN, as I am sure you are already aware, stands for International Standard Book Number, a 10-digit code that is the internationally recognized standard for identifying books and their various editions for over the past 30 years. You will also occasionally find a 9-digit code called simply the Standard Book Number, usually on books emanating from the early 1970s or thereabouts, and in many but not all of these cases you can "translate" the SBN into and ISBN by simply adding a leading zero.)

Listing a Book Manually On Amazon's Marketplace

1. ***Identify the ISBN and conduct a search*** for it by simply typing the number into any Amazon search box to determine if the book is in the Amazon.com catalogue. For our example, let's take a book of short fiction called ***A Day at the Ballpark, And Other Stories*** by Steve Holt. The ISBN is 0-7388-2395-3 and can be found, as is usually the case, both on the back cover above the bar code and on the copyright page inside the book. Exceptions to the back-cover placement are fairly common and include many hardcovers that display the ISBN inside the back dustjacket flap. Mass market paperbacks sometimes display the ISBN on the otherwise unprinted inside of the front cover, to facilitate processing of stripped-cover returns. You don't need to worry about including the hyphens or dashes when typing in an ISBN number at Amazon or Half.com.

Make sure, when your ISBN search yields results, that the edition listed is the edition you are preparing to sell. If there is a discrepancy between editions and their ISBN numbers, it is probably either because of an error by the publisher or because the edition you are preparing to sell is an advance reading copy, a Quality Paperback Book Club edition, or a hardcover book club edition. Even though such a discrepancy is not your fault, it is important to think about the prospective customer's point of view involving such discrepancies, and to avoid them. More often than not they will lead to disgruntled buyers, bad customer feedback, loss of time trying to explain yourself, and bad karma.

You may wonder how a publisher could possibly get its own ISBN number wrong. Unfortunately, the employees responsible for maintaining the ISBN logs for large publishers are often 23 year olds whose attention to detail leaves much to be desired. (Please excuse my reverse ageism, as I was not raised right). The result can often be more problematic than the failure to change an ISBN from the 5th edition to the 6th edition. We have seen many instances where the publishers' ISBN and edition information is out of synch for large print editions, book club editions, e-Book editions, and audio versions, and naturally this can cause just as much havoc for a buyer who is looking for a special version as the Marketplace sellers who regularly list their copies under the wrong ISBN in hopes of getting a better price. The point at which I resolved to increase my vigilance to ensure that such a discrepancy would never happen again in my business occurred as I was reading an angry email from a buyer who told me that she was nearly blind, had not received the large-print edition she had intended to order, and would never again order from a business which preyed on blind people to make a profit.

Occasionally the error is by the marketplace owner such as Amazon or Half.com, and in those cases using something like Amazon's A-to-Z Guarantee is certainly worth considering, but in most other cases, the best approach may be to make a full refund to the buyer upon receipt of the return.

- ***Check the list price and sales ranking.*** If the book comes up through your ISBN search, you now have access to very important information. As of this writing, you can see that ***A Day at the Ballpark*** is in stock at Amazon, by noting that its "Availability" reads "Usually ships within 24 hours". You can also see that Amazon does not ordinarily discount the book from its list price of $14.95, and that the book's Amazon Sales Ranking is 440,554, which means that, based on recent sales, it ranks in roughly the top 20% of all the books carried in the Amazon catalogue. This tells you that there is a trickle of demand for the book, but it is far from being a best seller: Amazon may be selling somewhere between half a dozen and a dozen ***new*** copies a month. It is important to realize that there are many books in Amazon's catalog that are not sold directly by Amazon, which obviously means that the buyer who wants such a book is very likely to buy it from you or from another Marketplace or zShop seller.

2. ***If the book does not come up through your ISBN search***, you can try searching by title, by clicking on "SEARCH" on the green link bar just below the search tabs at the top of your Amazon Books page. If you find your edition of the book in

Amazon's catalogue, you may continue following this guide; otherwise, set the book aside and see the next section in this chapter.

3. ***Check for other Marketplace copies*** by right-clicking on the "Used", "Collectible", or "New" links in the blue-bordered box labeled "MORE BUYING CHOICES" that will probably be placed right at the bottom of your first screen for ***A Day at the Ballpark***. This blue-bordered box is the starting point for all manual marketplace transactions by sellers or buyers. Using the right-click/"Open in New Window" function on your mouse will save you time and allow you to examine the price, condition, and number of listings by other Marketplace sellers for this title. At this writing, there are two listings for the book under "Used," priced at $7.95 and $8.99, one listing under "Collectible" offering a signed first edition for $15.00, and no Marketplace listings under "New." You may infer from this information that the book is relatively uncommon and that there is balance or equilibrium between sellers and buyers. But this also the time to go a little further in researching your competition. Take a quick glance at the number of customer-feedback stars for the sellers offering copies of the book: if they have part or all of the fifth star filled in in orange, they have decent or better feedback ratings and should be seen by you as competent and competitive, which means that if you are going to compete with them to sell your copy of the book, the means at your disposal are price, condition, and description. If they have four or fewer stars filled in, or an "I'm new" icon in place of the feedback stars, your feedback record may also help you compete in selling your book.

There are a few other important elements in researching the other copies available for sale. First, you may want to check to see if a seller has multiple copies for sale. This is not immediately obvious, and I must admit that I seldom check it unless there is a hint from the seller's store name, such as "Book Closeouts" or something along those lines, that the seller deals primarily in remainders. To check on this, click on a seller's storefront link, navigate to see their "Open listings" from his storefront or "About me" page, type or paste in the book's title, and search for it. When the title comes up, scroll down near the bottom of the web page and check quantity.

Second, you may want to check prices on other venues by navigating to Used.addall.com and doing a quick search for the book. At this writing the vast preponderance of books being sold on Amazon's Marketplace are available at cheaper prices elsewhere, with the exception of Amazon's penny-priced books that are constrained by the 75-cent price-limit at Half.com.

4. ***Click on the "Sell yours here" button*** at the bottom of the blue Marketplace box to begin listing your book. The next page that will appear on your screen is titled "Sell your item – Select Condition", and provides a pull-down menu where, referencing the earlier chapter titled "Grading and Describing Your Books," you must select the condition classification under which you will list the book and then click on the "Continue" button. The condition you select, of course, will have a bearing on the price you are able to get for the book.

5. ***Enter price, description, and seller preferences.*** The next page that comes up is called "Sell an item – Enter Price" but there are actually several other tasks here as well.

o   First, enter your description, referencing the earlier chapter titled "Grading and Describing Your Books". At this writing, Amazon's manual listing functionality still limits you to 70 characters in the description field for a copy classified as "Used".

o   Second, enter your price. Amazon may give you some price guidance on this page, although, interestingly, the categories of guidance appear to go through a cycling process and change from time to time. If Amazon sells the book itself, you will see a "Maximum Allowable Price" if you are listing a copy as "used" or "new", or a "Minimum Allowable Price" if you are listing a copy as "collectible." You may also see a "Recommended Price," an "Average Selling Price for This Item Based on Past Purchases," a "Seller's Price Guideline Based on Condition You Have Listed", or an "Average Price of Pre-Orders Based on Condition You Have Listed." Any of these can be helpful, but some are more helpful than others. It is clear that Amazon's Marketplace staff have struggled with issues related to the downward spiral of prices on common and hyper-common books, just as Marketplace sellers have. The experimentation with offering different kinds of pricing guidance for sellers speaks volumes about this. You will find a more thorough discussion of pricing strategies and the lowballing controversy further along in this book, but for now suffice it to say that the process of pricing most books for any marketplace, if there are already copies available on that marketplace, is usually, and certainly ought to be, a simple one. All other things being equal, including condition and feedback rating, your best chance at selling the book at the highest possible price is to have it appear as the first desirable listing that comes up when a potential buyer navigates to the page showing "used copies." You can accomplish this, at least for the moment, by pricing a book at the same price as the cheapest desirable copy available. If the book is a brisk seller, or is both desirable and in short supply, you may be able to go to a higher price level. There is no need to undercut the price of the cheapest available copy unless it is in better condition than the copy you are selling.

o   Remember: Amazon's interests are not the same as your interests here. All other things being equal, Amazon wants Marketplace sellers to sell the maximum possible number of books at the highest average price that buyers will pay. You, on the other hand, want to sell the maximum possible number of *your* books at the highest prices buyers will pay *to you.* If there are multiple copies of a book available at $7.95, in the same condition as yours from one or more sellers with as high a feedback rating as yours, and Amazon recommends that you price your copy at $11.89, they are making a recommendation based on their best interests rather than yours. Your best chance to sell *your* copy is at a price of $7.95 or below, and anyone who tells you differently is speculating, in a wildly inaccurate way, about buyer behavior.

Amazon.com price:	**$14.95**
Maximum allowable price:	**$14.95**
(Used items can not exceed the Amazon.com price)	
Recommended price:	**$11.89**
(Based on the condition you indicated)	
Average sales price for this item:	**$ 8.77**

(Based on past purchases)
Enter your price: **$7.95 US dollars**

6. Enter the *zip code* from which your item will be shipped. This will result in Amazon providing buyers with the state from which you ship, and some buyers may use shipping proximity as a basis for deciding which seller to buy from.

7. Select your *shipping methods*. You are required to offer "Standard Shipping" (4 to 14 business days) for which Amazon will credit you $2.23 (at this writing) based on the cost of a 3-pound package via USPS Media Mail. For all books that will fit into a USPS Priority Mail or Global Priority Mail large envelope flat, you should also check the other two options and offer both "Expedited Shipping" and "International Shipping." The vast majority of books will fit into these flat envelopes, and for those you will actually turn a profit on the shipping costs in many cases. For Expedited Shipments you should use USPS Priority Mail large flat envelopes (or your own packaging for shipments weighing less than one pound), and you will be reimbursed $4.35 for shipments that will cost you $3.85, or less if the item and its packaging weighs less than 13 ounces and can therefore be shipped via USPS First Class mail. For International Shipments, you will be reimbursed $8.95 each, and you should use either the large or small Global Priority Mail envelope. The large envelope costs $9 ($7 to Canada and Mexico) and the small envelope costs $5 ($4 to Canada and Mexico). Very rarely, you will have an international order from a country for which USPS does not offer Global Priority Mail, and you will then have to determine whether it is best to ship via air, via ground, or not at all. For more information on how to make sure that you do not lose money on Shipping and Handling, see the box under heading "Making Shipping & Handling Credits Work for You."

8. After you have selected your shipped methods and clicked on the "Continue" button at the bottom of the page, another

page will come up (it is the slowest loading page in the process), and on this page you will see the following entry areas:

- the quantity of copies you are posting under this listing (usually, but not always, "1");

- a SKU (stock keeping unit) number (see the chapter titled "Organizing Your Physical Inventory");

- under "Add a Picture", there is no need to make any entry if you are listing the item on Marketplace. (If you are listing an item on zShops only, this is where you can upload a digital image of your item.);

- under "Choose Your zShops Real Estate," you will find a pulldown menu under "Books" to allow you to select a category. If you are listing under Marketplace, you may want to save time by clicking on "Other," since there is little benefit to better zShops searchability if your title is already going to come up through an Amazon search, linked to Amazon's main page for the item.

- At the bottom of this page, I suggest that you click the box that reads "Feature on your zShops Storefront" but, if you are listing in Marketplace, ignore the field for "zShops Storefront Browse Path."

9. You are almost done. Just click on the "Continue" button at the bottom of the page, and the next page that will come up will allow you to review your submission and click on "Submit." At that point, your item is in the pipeline toward being listed, and may be available for purchase within minutes, or it may take as long as 24 hours.

By now, you are well aware that there are plenty of other venues where you may wish to list your books, and that you also have the option of listing books in a more "automated" fashion at Amazon and elsewhere by using Amazon's Inventory Loader or Book Loader or other software programs or functionalities such as BookTrakker,

BookHound, Homebase, BookRouter, or Price Hunter. But before you move into using any of these options, I recommend that you put yourself through the valuable experience of listing several hundred books manually at Amazon. The experience can teach a lot about writing good descriptions, pricing books well and fairly, figuring out what books to acquire, and other fine points of online bookselling. And it will also prepare you to work more efficiently and effectively when you deem yourself ready to try automated listing. We'd love to be able to provide some direction in that process, but with software changing as quickly as it does we can only suggest the following:

- Read directions and instructions carefully and follow them closely;

- Check your work often in the early going by trying uploads of a few titles at a time so that you know that you are doing things the right way before you invest too much of your time; and

- Don't be bashful about asking for help; with the exception of Price Hunter, the software providers and website staff involved with these programs are very experienced at holding hands with literate cyber-illiterates as we learn our way.

X   Maintaining & Using Your Book Repair Toolbox

Used booksellers move very quickly at library sales, yard sales, thrift shops and other such haunts, and sometimes find out later that some of the great titles they picked up have flaws. So what do you do with a book that has a few tears, a label's residue on the cover, or even a musty smell? You could list it as "Acceptable" and ensure either that it will not sell or that it will sell to somebody who doesn't read the listing and will complain about its condition. You could toss it out or donate it back to the library whence you bought it. But in many cases there is a better solution:

Yes, it's time to get out your trusty *bookseller's repair toolbox*!

There are probably as many different approaches to book repair, and as many different tools in use, as there are experienced used booksellers, but it will come as no surprise that the best efforts to codify the art of book repair have come from librarian. We therefore recommend that you avail yourself of these truly impressive and rather amazing online authorities on the subject:

• Book Repair, by Elizabeth Dodds, Colby College Libraries (www.colby.edu/library/collections/technical_services/wp/BookRepair.html)

• A Simple Book Repair Manual, Preservation Services, Dartmouth College Library (http://www.dartmouth.edu/~preserve/repair/repairindex.htm)

• Emergency Salvage of Moldy Books and Paper, by Beth Lindblom Patkus, Northeast Document Conservation Center (http://www.nedcc.org/plam3/tleaf39.htm)

Your Book Repair Toolbox

Meanwhile, here are a few good suggestions both from our own experience and that of other sellers, for items that you may want to keep in a very basic book repair toolbox:

• *Goo Gone* is a widely used solvent known for doing wonders when it comes to cleaning book cover residue. You can probably pick it up at your neighborhood hardware or art supplies store, or find an exhaustive list of physical and mail-order retailers at the website of its manufacturer, **Magic American** (www.magicamerican.com). The website is worth a trip even if you already have a supply and a source, if only to read customer testimonials like "When I discovered Goo Gone, my whole world changed" and "If it had been a commercial, I would have sworn it was faked!"

• Another product that has received strong bookseller testimonials for its power to clean residue and soiling is **Whisper Kleen**, manufactured by BondRite and available at industrial supply distributors including Southeastern Distribution (800-825-1444).

• *White paper hinge tape* and/or other book repair tapes from the library suppliers *Highsmith* (www.highsmith.com) and *Brodart* (www.brodart.com). Indeed, it's well worth your time to go to both of these sites and browse around under their "Library Supplies" and "Book Repair" headings.

• An *exacto knife* or something similar.

• You will need a *book press* if you regularly deal with seriously warped hardcover books that will have some value if you can get them straightened out. But before you go spending money for the real thing, you may want to try a little creative substitution with a *tennis racket press*. Or, if you have some very rudimentary carpentry skills and a power drill, you can make your own book press out of two boards and four long bolts held by wing nuts.

• If a book has labels or stickers than do not readily come off, try warming them with a *hair dryer* and you will probably be able to remove them more easily.

• While most booksellers will agree that it is far better to avoid any book with a musty order than to deodorize it, because *mildew spreads,* there may well be times when you want to try to salvage such a book, and such times will demand the elements of your own

book deodorizing kit, including resealable bags, some form of "separator", and an appropriate solution. Most solutions involve mothballs, which of course have their own toxicity, but you may want to try the solution offered by our colleagues at J Godsey Booksellers (email: gods@attbi.com), who sell Book Deodorizing granules by the quart for $12.50 postpaid with a money back guarantee: "The granules are a dry solid clay base permeated with a minute amount of a deodorizing chemical that is not reactive to dry porous materials such as books, paper and textiles. They work best when enclosed in a plastic airtight container such as a bag or plastic box for a period of time relative to the severity of the odor. About a week or two for stuffy, mildew smells. The residual odor dissipates with a few hours airing."

- Several clean, high-quality art gum and other ***erasers*** of the kind you can buy at an art supplies store will come in handy when removing pencil and other marks, scribbles, prices, and marginalia.

- A ***ruler***

- ***Rubber bands***

- ***Scissors***

- ***Clean rags***

If you have the kind of love for books that inspires many of us to situate ourselves in this line of work, you will probably find a special pleasure in the arts of repairing books. Keeping a good book in circulation a while longer and making it into a more attractive purchase for its next buyer is well worth the expenditure of your time and energy even if it doesn't always translate into a good hourly rate of profit.

XI   Business Priorities And Organization

Now that you have addressed other important issues such as finding good inventory and sourcing your business' key goods and services, and pricing, describing, and posting your books online, let's **really** get down to brass tacks. It is my firm belief that **nobody** should try to operate a small business without a clear understanding of, and quantifiable answers to, the three key business questions that follow.

The Three Key Business Questions

• **What is your break-even?** Chances are, if you are operating out of your home, that you have very few business-related fixed expenses that must be paid regardless of how many books you sell and what you get for them. But you probably have a few, and one of the first things you should do is to list them, total them, and determine what is your break-even budget: how much revenue do you need to bring in each month to generate enough profit to pay these fixed costs?   To set up a useful, interactive "what if" spreadsheet that will allow you to project your break-even as well as other outcomes "for better or worse," use the Table called "Determining Your Break-Even Point."

• **What are your long-term goals?** Ultimately, do you intend for your efforts to be a hobby, to provide a nice part-time income, to give you a living wage, or to make you a prosperous, successful professional? I suggest that you use the Table entitled "Projecting a Business Plan" as a beginning point to set some goals for yourself and to help you decide exactly what you want to get out of the work you put into your business. The definitions of what is a part-time income, a living wage, or a prosperous professional's rewards may vary greatly based on where you live, what stage of life you are at, and what your financial responsibilities are, so don't settle for our guidelines if you feel you can improve upon them. But whatever you do, don't succumb to the cop-out of setting no goals at all. Building in some quantifiable expectations will allow you to give yourself a pat

Table 2: Determining Your Break-even Point

Step 1: List and total your monthly fixed costs
Monthly Fixed Costs

Phone line including all taxes and fees	$38.16
Online ISP monthly charge ($10 to $24)	$23.90
Internet Postage account ($9.95 to $15)	$14.95
Amazon monthly Pro Merchant fee*	$39.99
Total (A)	$117.00

Step 2: Estimate average cost of goods sold
Example: if all your books cost you $1 each and you sold them for $5 each, your COGS would be 20%

Average cost of goods sold (B)	20%

Step 3: Apply this formula to arrive at your break-even revenue: C=A x (1/(1-(15%+B)))

Gross Sales necessary to generate break-even gross profit* (C)	**$180.00**

or, to re-state this as an Operating Statement:

Operating Statement

Gross Sales	$180.00
Amazon Transaction Fee	$27.00
Net Sales	$153.00
Less Cost of Goods Sold	$36.00
Gross Profit	$117.00
Less Operating Expense	$117.00
Net Profit	**$0.00**

A 20% COGS and a 15% average transaction fee means, of course, that your gross profit will be 65%. Does this mean that 65% of all of your revenues beyond your break-even point will be sheer profit? Perhaps, but probably not. It is more likely that, as you acquire and sell more books, you will also be experiencing expenses such as travel costs to go to book sales. But you should have a good handle on your break-even budget so that you know what you are building upon.

*The figures above are based on having an Amazon Pro Merchant account (a must if you sell 10 books a week!) and on the notion that your "shipping & handling" costs are a break-even expense with the shipping credits you receive from Amazon.com and Half.com. This should be easy to achieve; see Table 1: Making Shipping & Handling Credits Work for You.

on the back if you reach them, to decide that you need to strengthen your business plan if you fall short, and perhaps to move on into a more suitable endeavor if you determine that you have been wildly unrealistic.

*   ***What are the "metrics" necessary to meet your long-term goals?*** If you've left a high-powered corporate environment to work out of your home, thinking in terms of performance "metrics" or "benchmarks" may be the last thing you want to do. But if you are seriously committed to making a go of it, you owe it to yourself to translate your overall business goals into some very specific and concrete performance goals, and that's what metrics are. Using the "Business Metrics" worksheet, try to translate your business goals into yearly, monthly, weekly, and daily benchmarks for number of books sold, total dollars sold, size of inventory in units, size of inventory in dollars, number of books listed, dollar value of books listed, and number and value of books acquired for listing. If you don't set goals and translate them into metrics, you'll never know if you are succeeding or failing.

Once you have done the work to address these questions – either on your own, or with the help of the aforementioned tables, or with an accountant's help – you should find it relatively simple and straightforward to review, refresh, and update your approach to these questions on a regular basis. How often is "a regular basis"? Well, your obligations to the government require you to address your financial performance only once a quarter (for estimated tax payments) or once a year (for income tax returns), but that's not enough. You need to stay tuned in to market changes and to your own performance so that you can be quick on your feet when it comes to tweaking your business model or strengthening your inventory, market plan, or competitive edge. One of the approaches that will help you stay tuned in to what's important is to review these three key business questions monthly or even weekly.

These are just a few fundamental questions where your ability to provide yourself with good direction and helpful answers will depend greatly upon your ability to maintain accurate business records and organize them in useful ways. If your business is growing and you'd like to explore other ways of making financial record-keeping work for you, I suggest that you pick up a copy of a very good book called *Managing by the Numbers : A Commonsense Guide to Understanding and Using Your Company's Financials: An Essential Resource for Growing Businesses* by Chuck Kremer and Ron Rizzuto (Perseus Press: 2000; ISBN: 0738202568).

Organizing Your Business

Running a small business can become an administrative nightmare if you allow things to get out of hand, but there's no need for you to allow it. Taking a few simple steps early on can go a long way in helping you avoid unnecessary problems later. So I'll start with these suggestions:

• Maintain some physical separation between your business life and your home life. To the extent that space allows, this might mean separate desks, separate "in-boxes" for mail, separate bank accounts, separate rooms in your house, and that sort of thing.

• Even if you plan to have an accountant or tax service do your taxes, I recommend that you make use of a relatively cheap, popular business software program such as Quickbooks or Quicken. I mention these two from Intuit specifically because, while there are plenty of other good accounting programs, these two are so ubiquitous that they have become the standards, and using them should mean relative ease when it comes to downloading and uploading your business files between them and your online bank account, on the one hand, and any tax preparation software you may decide to use, on the other.

• Organize your business from the beginning as a sole proprietorship, pay attention to your tax obligations, and organize your record-keeping, financial reports, and financial projections from the beginning to be driven by your tax reporting obligations as you'll find them in Schedule C (see below).

• Spend at least 15 minutes a day on your business finances and you'll save yourself dozens of hours later.

• Look for every available opportunity to run your business on-line, using an online bank account, a well-organized email system, a software program such as Quickbooks, and either someone else's software products or your own system of spreadsheets for inventory and fulfillment record-keeping, and one of the online postage and shipping programs like Endicia. It just doesn't make sense to run an internet selling business out of shoeboxes of paper when its elements become more and more computer-friendly every day.

Licenses and Legalities

Organize your business from the beginning, or from now on, to operate properly under the applicable business laws. This means, for starters:

• Maintain accurate and complete financial records necessary to file federal and state income taxes for your business, and file and pay these taxes on time.

• Maintain accurate and complete financial records necessary to file state sales taxes for your business, and file and pay these taxes on time. In all likelihood, this will mean paying sales taxes only on the sales to customers who reside in the same state as you, since you are probably maintaining an office or business place only in the state where you reside. Having a state sales tax certificate will also provide you with the documentation you will need to forego paying a sales tax when you buy books at library sales and used bookstores.

• Register your business with any authorities that require such registration. The best place to start is your town clerk's office and the website for your state revenue department. Such registration or licensing may result in fees roughly equivalent to a month or two of Amazon Pro Merchant fees, but compliance with the law is always the best policy. Those of us who conduct our business online should never make the mistake of assuming that the laws don't apply to us because our businesses are somehow invisible. Among the several reasons this is true is that such presumed "invisibility", if it *is* the case today, will probably not be the case for long.

Insurance

There are several different varieties of insurance to think about here, and of course each of them may involve a choice between spending money and going without. Maybe you've been thinking of your enterprise as a hobby in many ways, but if it is providing all or a significant part of your income and it represents your primary plan for the future economically speaking, you need to guard against unforeseen catastrophes. You should certainly start by trying to get the most out of the money you are already spending, but don't reject out of hand the possibility that you may need to spend some money on several different kinds of insurance. Although these costs may be higher at first blush than your current insurance costs, remember that your business insurance costs are fully deductible business expenses, so that you may end up with a net savings after all.

Health insurance is probably the single most important element in the economic safety net of any individual or family, and if you have any way of continuing health coverage either directly or through a spouse or domestic partner, give serious consideration to doing that. If you or your partner is leaving the day job, you may be able to continue health coverage temporarily under the provisions of the COBRA Ac t of 1986, but that can become very expensive very quickly. You may also want to investigate group health insurance coverage plans available through organizations such as the Independent Online Booksellers Association, the American Booksellers Association or its regional affiliate in your area, or your regional or local small business association.

One of the primary reasons for keeping your day job is health insurance. One of these days somebody will figure out a great way to provide health insurance at reasonable rates to independent home-based entrepreneurs like many of us, but until that happens, we may have to rely on our day jobs or the day jobs of our spouses or domestic partners – boy, aren't we up-to-the-minute here? – to meet our health insurance needs if they are going to be met.

Property insurance may not seem important at first if you are spending hours posting books that only cost you a quarter a piece, but one day you may well look up and realize that the total listed value of your inventory amounts to $25,000, $50,000, or perhaps even more. It's unlikely that your inventory will be stolen, but a flood or a fire could knock you out of business overnight. If you work out of space that you have already insured with homeowner's or renter's insurance, it makes sense to begin by having a candid conversation with your agent to see whether provisions can be made within your existing policy to meet your insurance needs. But it may also be well worth your time to speak to a business insurance agent – possibly, of course, this will be the same agent – to explore the potential costs and benefits of property insurance, business interruption insurance, liability insurance, and disability insurance. You are your own boss and it is up to you to decide what's important and what will give you peace of mind. Whatever you do, don't make the mistake of hiding the fact that you have been running a home business from your property insurer. The likely effect of such deception, should you need to file a claim, will be that the claim will not be honored. If you are working out of your home, you should be consistent in the calculations you make about space and expenses allotted to the home business, and make sure that you use the same calculations for insurance and tax purposes.

Automobile insurance is also worth a new look in light of your business enterprise. The use of your automobile to go on book-buying trips near and far and to take your shipping to the post office on a regular basis will likely have effects on your auto insurance policy, the way you treat the vehicle for tax purposes, and possibly even the vehicle classification under which you register the vehicle. A good personal auto insurance agent should be able to help you determine whether you ought to classify you automobile as a commercial vehicle either because it is a requirement or because it is a beneficial option. In any case, when it comes time to do your taxes, you will be able to depreciate part of the value of your automobile and to take various deductions because part of your use is related to the operation of your business.

XII   Fulfillment And Customer Service

Okay, you've started to build an inventory, listed your books, and seen your first sales come through. That's the fun part. Now comes the part where you earn the money you are making.

In order to succeed at online bookselling, it is absolutely necessary that you establish a consistent daily routine for confirming and fulfilling customer orders. It may be possible to limit the routine to every other day if sales are slow and your other responsibilities dictate, but tending to these chores daily is better because it will allow you to fulfill orders more promptly, stay ahead of any problems that may arise, and avoid needing to do the kind of mountain of fulfillment work that will rise to greet you on Monday morning if you have a brisk sales weekend and you haven't focused on fulfillment since Friday morning. Whatever your approach, try to ship as many as possible of your orders within 24 hours, and your customers will love you for your promptness. Amazon Marketplace or zShop sellers are required to ship within two business days of an order's receipt, and at Half.com sellers are required to confirm all orders within two business days and then to ship within one business day of confirmation. But you shouldn't settle for being "as good as you have to be," when you can be "as good as you can be," without any more work.

Try to make your shipping routine as simple, sensible, and automated as possible. You can rely if you wish on the "Sold and Ship" emails you receive from Amazon and other venues, or in Amazon's case you also have the option of downloading a fulfillment report that you can open into Microsoft Excel.

If you are going to use a downloadable fulfillment report, you'll also be able to create or download a system of prebuilt spreadsheets that will automatically take your daily fulfillment reports and turn them into picking lists, packing slips, and even daily financial reports. If you have sufficient familiarity with Microsoft Excel you may be able to create such a spreadsheet system yourself. If you prefer to purchase a relatively inexpensive software application that will take care of this for you, just send an email with contact information to OnlineBookselling@nativeweb.net.

A Daily Routine

Downloading a Fulfillment Report

- Go to <u>Your seller account</u> *(from your "Your account" page, of course)*
- On the <u>Your seller account</u> *page, under Your Inventory, click on* <u>Download fulfillment and listings reports</u>
- *When this page comes up, click on* <u>Generate reports now</u>
- *When prompted, give your password*
- *On the* Generate Reports Now *page that comes up next, scroll down to* Order Fulfillment Report, *click on "Yes" and click on the "Preview" button at the bottom of the page*
- *On the next page, click on the* Generate Reports Now *button*
- *On the* <u>Your seller account</u> *page, under Your Inventory, click on* <u>Download fulfillment and listings reports</u>
- *When this page comes up, click on* <u>Pickup generated reports</u>
- *On the* Pickup Generated Reports *page that comes up next, click on the* Order Fulfillment Report *for the current date when it appears (You should get an email with the title* Notification of Order Fulfillment Report Completion *when the report is ready to download, or you can check by refreshing the "pickup" page from time to time; these reports usually appear within 15 minutes of your request)*

In response to prompts, download and save the file in a place where you will be able to locate it on your computer, with a file name you will recognize. When you are given a prompt that the download is complete, open it with Microsoft Excel, and then re-save it as a spreadsheet. You will then be able to make a copy of it and edit as you wish for other purposes.

Using these tools, we follow a very simple and straightforward daily routine here at Windwalker Books:

1. Download a daily fulfillment report from Amazon

2. For other selling venues, aggregate all order emails into Microsoft Word file

3. Respond to customer service email messages and issues

4. Print out a "picking list" of all titles to be shipped today and pick the books

5. Prepare the day's books for shipping, take a final look at condition and check back against the listing condition if there is any question

6. Package and weigh each book and create a postage-paid shipping label for each book using www.Endicia.com. Endicia will pick up a mailing address automatically, directly from a "Sold" email or from your downloaded fulfillment report spreadsheet. All you have to do is "select" the address with your mouse, then right-click and select "Copy", and the mailing address will be transferred magically to your next Endicia label screen.

7. Deliver the books to the post office where you should be allowed to drop them off without waiting in line

8. Once the day's shipments have been dropped at the post office, send out confirmation emails to the customers

9. Post 25 new titles to our inventory

10. Review/refresh/reprice/update at least 25 "older" titles

Three other tasks that need attention several times a week, but not necessarily every day, have little to do with fulfillment. Yet they are very important to running a thriving, well-organized online bookshop:

- Buy books (See Chapter 5)

- Organize your inventory – a few minutes every other day spent straightening, dusting, consolidating, etc., will guard against disorganization and also against erosion of condition

- Check the "industry news". There are several easy ways to keep up with the important news that affects you as a bookseller and the bookselling industry in general. If you sell on Amazon's Marketplace you should use the links provided on the right-hand side of your seller page to check the Seller Announcement message board and the Seller Connection message board daily. To keep up with book trade news, register for free online access to the New York Times and sign up for subject-driven email alerts for "Book Trade" articles. You may also want to consider subscribing to one or both of two pertinent "mailing lists" – the *Bookfinder Insider* list that can be accessed at www.bookfinder.com and the *Bibliophile* list at www.bibliophilegroup.com. But readers beware! Don't allow your self to start spending large portions of your precious time chewing the fat or trying to become a message board star.

Packaging

Since the events involving postal packages that occurred after September 11, 2001, it has become more important than ever for booksellers to follow packaging guidelines to help prevent inquiries, misunderstandings, and delays associated with book shipments. The following guidelines are drawn from the Amazon Marketplace site, but with a few changed words they could apply equally well to shipments associated with any bookselling venue:

- Prepare a professional, clean package. Use new shipping/packing materials intended for packing items like yours. Avoid the use of drying materials or similar substances. Seal all shipments tightly and be sure to wipe away any dust or debris that may have collected on the item before packing for delivery.

- Use a complete return address on all packages, printed in a neat and legible manner. Include your seller name in the return address.

- The use of metered postage is recommended. Avoid excessive postage and the use of small denomination postage stamps.

- Prominently label the package with the message, "Your Amazon.com Marketplace Order" (or Auctions or zShops).

- Include the packing slip provided in your "Sold--ship now!" e-mail, or a similar written reminder of the transaction details, with your item.

If you are shipping a book or books with very high value, you may want to consider packaging either in a shipping box with bubblewrap inside or in the kind of safe and secure packaging solution being offered by *TransparentMail* (www.transparentmail.com). But for most book shipments in the under-$20 range, padded mailers such as the ones we buy from Associated Bag (www.associatedbag.com, see Chapter IV) do fine. We have shipped tens of thousands of books in this form of packaging without ever receiving a packaging-related customer complaint.

Confirmation Emails

Try to keep your *confirmation letters* brief, helpful, and a little bit informal. Buyers seems to appreciate the proper balance of friendly helpfulness, information, and professionalism, and a good initial contact can help to inoculate your relationship against hard feelings and bad feedback if a problem develops either because the customer ordered the wrong edition or the delivery of your shipment was slower than usual.

Note, in the table at the left, that Margaret's email confirmation message includes the delivery confirmation number right off of Endicia or USPS Shipping Assistant. Personally I like this touch and the fact that it gives the buyer some peace of mind, but some sellers avoid giving out Delivery Confirmation information in the confirmation email because they fear both that buyers will not understand the distinction between a Delivery Confirmation Number and a Tracking Number (DC does not ordinarily provide the same tracking detail that is available with true tracking), and also

A Great Confirmation Email

We've ordered dozens of books from other third-party sellers, and still count this email, excerpted here with the permission of CyberSolutions' Margaret Craig (www.amazon.com/shops/cybersolutions) as the best confirmation email we have ever received:

Thanks so very much for your purchase! I received your order confirmation today for your Amazon.com Marketplace purchase and your item was shipped today by way of Media Mail with delivery confirmation # 0280 5213 9070 1234 5678. Shipment can be confirmed at www.usps.com or by calling 1-800-222-1811.

Media Mail can take 4-14 business days and in some cases outside the continental US to take up to 30 days
Priority Mail is expected to arrive in 2-3 days but is not guaranteed.
Global Priority is expected to arrive in 4-7 days but is not guaranteed.

Packages mailed to destinations outside the continental US can take longer than 21 days and can take as long as 30 days to arrive such as Hawaii, Alaska and APO, AE or FPO. (Even Priority Mail). Keep in mind that all deliveries, even Priority Mail may be delayed due to added security measures.

If for any reason your buying experience was not enjoyable, please e-mail me at msc5866@aol.com first to resolve and I will do whatever I can do to correct the problem if possible. Your satisfaction is my main concern. Comments on your buying experience with me can be left by going to www.amazon.com/buyer-feedback

Thanks again for your purchase and I hope to do business with you again in the future. If you would like to check out all my other items for sale, please go to: http://amazon.com/shops/cyber-solutions or feel free to e-mail me as I may have items not yet listed or that are listed on a site other than Amazon. Or if I do not have the item, I could possibly help you find what you are looking for.

Margaret Craig
Cyber Solutions

because Delivery Confirmation only confirms that the package was delivered, not that it was delivered correctly.

Customer Service

Once you have completed your confirmation messages, your contact with the customer is complete in the vast majority of cases. But occasionally a problem will arise, and over time you will find that your business will run much more smoothly if you develop a consistent, friendly, and focused approach to all customer service issues and apply it without prejudice or any negative attitude. Even though you may pour your heart and soul into your business, it will do you no good to take customer service issues personally. Having a consistent approach and a clear customer service policy will help you to maintain a friendly demeanor with all your customers and to avoid stewing over the more difficult ones.

A well thought out approach to customer service ought to include several public pronouncements that are clearly stated in appropriate places such as your Amazon Marketplace storefront and several internal policies to back them up. For public consumption, you should address the following, and rather than suggesting specific language here I recommend you review other storefronts' policies for a sense of what works and what appeals to you, and then decide what will work for you:

• Packaging and condition: Let your customers know that you will take care in packaging their books and that you adhere to high standards for rating and describing your books. If you are a member of any trade associations you may want to post this information as well, since it can help to reassure prospective buyers that they are dealing with a professional.

• Promptness. If you are able to ship every order within 24 hours of its receipt, this is an important commitment to share with your customers.

Returns and Refunds. Prospective buyers often want to know up front that they have the right to return items if they are not satisfied. Sometimes booksellers are hesitant to "lead with their chin" when it comes to proclaiming a "No Questions Asked" return policy because they are fearful they will become target practice for unscrupulous buyers, but with very rare exceptions book buyers are a fair and friendly bunch who are unlikely to try to take advantage of booksellers. The best practice is to clearly state a balanced returns policy so that customers know what will be expected of them in order to obtain a refund, and also know that they can expect that refund promptly if they meet these responsibilities. Frequently you may feel that a customer is seeking a refund to redress a mistake that really was his own responsibility, but in most cases it is simply not worth the time, effort, and money to argue with a customer after an initial statement of your point of view. If you feel that an Amazon

---

Dealing with Incorrect Addresses

If you use www.Endicia.com or another Internet postage provider, you will be required to verify a buyer's address electronically and automatically in the process of printing your label. Once in a great while, the buyer address that is transmitted to you through Amazon, Half.com, eBay or another venue will be unverifiable through the post office. If this happens, here are a few suggestions:

- Check first to see if the address is formatted correctly: truncated street address lines and apartment numbers or corporate names in the "wrong place" sometimes seem to stump the USPS computer.

- Email the customer to verify the ship-to address, and don't fret if it takes the customer a couple days to get back to you. Sometimes buyers take a vacation, sometimes they only use a computer at the office, and in any case they are usually less likely to spend as much time online as you are. If they get back to you and verify the address is accurate, you may just have to go back to the 20th century and ship the item manually.

- If a buyer does not respond to email, try sending a quick postcard asking that he contact you immediately to verify the address. This is what you would do if you were L.L. Bean, so try it.

- If none of these approaches works, it's time to cancel and refund the order. Include a nice note in the refund message field, spell out your willingness to hold the item for a few days in case you hear from the buyer, and also give a call or email to Customer Service to the venue that transmitted the bad address to you, so as to document the situation in the event of bad feedback or a complaint.

Marketplace buyer is blatantly trying to defraud you, you have the option of directing them to Amazon's A-to-Z Guarantee program where they may seek a refund directly from Amazon. In such cases it is important to document your communications and to be prepared to respond in a non-defensive fashion to Amazon's inquiries to you. Using the A-to-Z Guarantee program is especially important if you suspect that a buyer is carrying out a pattern of internet fraud and is likely to victimize other sellers, because Amazon maintains records on these buyers and has been known to enforce a "three strikes and your out" policy with respect to buyers.

• Reshipments. If a buyer claims that a shipment has not arrived in a reasonable period of time, much of the time you will find that the buyer is looking not for a refund but for the book. In such cases you should have a policy that calls for you to verify the shipping address, to ask the customer to check both with his local post office and elsewhere in his building if there is any chance that the shipment is being held in a office mailroom or by a neighbor. If you are then able to offer the customer a re-shipment either from your existing stock or by getting a colleague to drop-ship for you, this may be the best outcome for all concerned.

• Communication. E-mail your buyers when you ship their item (see section on Confirmation Emails" above). Let them know it is on the way, and by what method you have shipped it. If you drop-ship or are shipping from an address or city unfamiliar to your buyer, notify them via e-mail of the package origin or "ship from" address. Keep in mind that deliveries may be delayed because of added security measures. Above all, keep communicating with a buyer who is concerned about a shipping delay or lost item, and make it easy for the buyer to keep communicating with you.

Customer Feedback and Customer Complaints

Entire bookshelves full of books have been written about the basic fact that e-Commerce accentuates the importance of customer service because the Internet is so transparent that a few disgruntled customers can really do a job on the reputation of any online business, and the same is true for online bookselling. It is absolutely essential to excel consistently when it comes to four basic issues: condition, packaging, shipping time, and communication. If you excel at these, you will almost definitely be able to maintain a good strong customer feedback record that will be visible to prospective buyers on Amazon Marketplace, eBay, or Half.com if you sell on these venues.

However, be prepared for the likelihood that only somewhere between 5 and 10 per cent of your customers will leave feedback for you, and among these most sellers believe that the disgruntled customer is far more likely to leave feedback than the satisfied customer. Consequently, sellers frequently try out various strategies for improving their feedback by increasing the percentage of satisfied customers who leave feedback and even by trying to suppress the percentage of disgruntled customers who leave feedback. There are also plenty of sellers who consider it unseemly to lobby for feedback in any way. As you determine how you'd like to approach this question of business culture, you may want to consider some of the approaches that sellers have taken to influence their customer feedback ratings and provide a little "spin control" for negative ratings:

- Include a request for customer feedback in confirmations emails.

- Using the Endicia Postage Log status reports to confirm shipment arrivals, send another "arrival confirmation" email immediately after a customer has received his shipment, and include a request for customer feedback.

- Respond to feedback on their online storefronts, explaining any negative feedback or misunderstandings.

- Respond to buyer's feedback with email.

- Respond to buyer's feedback with feedback on the buyer.

All this being said, the best way to deal with negative feedback is to avoid getting it. At the first sign of a problem involving a buyer, you should shift into high gear to pre-empt problems and to bowl your buyer over being disarmingly gracious and understanding while responding promptly in a friendly and thorough manner to every contact. As a result of these efforts you will receive better feedback and more sales, and the small time or expense involved in sending a few emails or even making a refund or reshipment will be more than offset by better sales and fewer complaints in the future. All other things being equal, a higher feedback rating translates into more sales, and a poor feedback rating translates into more questions and complaints as buyers become more easily concerned at any hint of a problem and are less likely to give a seller the benefit of the doubt if a Media Mail shipment takes a few extra days.

XIII   Taxes And Other Perks

If you are just beginning in this business, or if you have been at it for a while but have never paid much attention to its tax implications beyond paying taxes on your revenues, this is where I get to share some ***very good news*** with you.

One of the largest and most financially powerful organizations in the world wants to help you in some very significant ways that will not only improve your business and household bottom lines, but also stand a good chance to improve your quality of life.

You guessed it. It's the United States Internal Revenue Service that wants to help, and probably your state's department of revenue or taxation as well. How?

Have you been deducting the business expense for the van or car that you use to schlep books around? It's time to start.

Have you been using IRS Form 8829 to deduct the "Business Use of Your Home" cost of the garage or basement or study or extra bedroom area where your store and ship your books and otherwise run your business? It's time to start.

Have you been deducting the expense of your book purchases at yard sales, library sales, used bookshops, and all the other places where you acquire your inventory, as well as your expenses in traveling to and fro? It's time to start.

And what was that I said about quality of life? Well, there's a good chance, if you are in this line of work, that you and possibly even your partner really enjoy finding out of the way used bookshops and thrift shops and whiling away the hours searching out treasures in them. From now on, please accept this encouragement to plan your future vacations around these activities whenever possible, to keep detailed notes of your book explorations along the way and to keep equally detailed records of you're the business expenses you incur in the process. With careful planning, you will be able to stretch your vacation dollar another 20 per cent or so, and chances

Table 3: Organizing Your Business for Schedule C

The Internal Revenue Service Schedule C (Profit or Loss from Business - Sole Proprietorship) is the form on which you will file your income taxes with the government, and the bottom line from Schedule C will go right onto your Form 1040. You will save yourself a great deal of time and money down the road if you organize your business and track your expense categories from the beginning to mesh with Schedule C. The categories are listed here as they appear on Schedule C, and those that that are most germane to the used bookselling business are discussed in greater detail on the following pages. Also, pay special attention the following table for Form 8829, Expenses for Business Use of Your Home.

Part I   Income
1 Gross receipts or sales
2 Returns and allowances
3 Subtract line 2 from line 1
4 Cost of goods sold (from line 42)
5 Gross profit (subtract line 4 from line 3)
6 Other income
7 Gross income
Part II   Expenses
8 Advertising
9 Bad debts from sales or services
10 Car and truck expenses
11 Commissions and fees
12 Depletion
13 Depreciation
14 Employee benefit programs
15 Insurance (other than health)
16 Interest
    a Mortgage
    b Other
17 Legal & professional services
18 Office expense
19 Pension & profit-sharing plans
20 Rent or lease
    a Vehicles, machinery, equip.
    b Other business property

21 Repairs and maintenance
22 Supplies (not included in Part III)
23 Taxes and licenses
24 Travel, meals, and entertainment
    a Travel
    b Meals and entertainment
25 Utilities
26 Wages
27 Other expense
28 Total expenses
29 Tentative profit (loss)
30 Expenses for business use of your home (Attach Form 8829)
31 Net profit or (loss)
Part III   Cost of Goods Sold
35 Inventory at beginning of year
36 Purchases less cost of items withdrawn for personal use
37 Cost of labor
38 Materials and supplies
39 Other costs
40 Add lines 35 through 39
41 Inventory at end of year
42 Cost of goods sold
Part V   Other Expenses
Bank charges
Online charges
Telephone

are it will be great for your bookselling inventory *and* your mental health.

Protecting Yourself

As important as it is to take the deductions you have coming as a small business owner, it is equally important to protect yourself both by making sure you keep accurate records and also by knowing what you will need if an expense or deduction is questioned by the IRS or your state taxation agency. Here are some suggestions that may save you headaches and money down the road:

• Keep in mind that, for instance, if the IRS decides to challenge your deductions for your *use of your home for business purposes,* it is unlikely that it will happen right away. Often such inquiries begin two or three years after the tax return in question, and in rare cases even longer. Two or three years from now your use of space for your business may be entirely different than it is now, if you even continue to operate the business! If you can't prove to the IRS how you used the space that led to your deduction, you stand a good chance of seeing that deduction disallowed. The best way to protect yourself against such an unhappy turn of events is to *take photographs* of all the space in question, and keep them on hand and well-filed so that you will be able to make your case if you ever need to do so. And also keep in mind the IRS requirement that, to qualify for a home business deduction, an area of your home must have been used *exclusively* for business purposes.

• If you make regular donations of unwanted books to libraries, schools, or charities, you will want to be able to make deductions for those donations. You may only be donating a few books at a time, but they could well add up to a significant amount of money by the end of the year. The IRS has very specific rules covering charitable contributions, and to begin with you must obtain written acknowledgement of your contributions for the recipient organization anytime your donations to such an organization total $250 or more during a single tax year. You'll be in much better shape if you print out a simple receipt form with blank spaces for number of books, their value (which should equal their cost to you), the date,

Table 4: Expenses for Business Use of Your Home

Tne Internal Revenue Service Form 8829 (Expenses for Business Use of Your Home) is the form that allows you to make significant income tax deductions for the portion of your home that is used solely for your business. If you run all or part of your business from your home, it's important to organize your business finances from the beginning so that they mesh not only with the categories on Schedule C, but also with Form 8829. It is also crucially important to maintain the greatest possible degree of physical separation between the space you devote strictly to your business operations and the rest of your home, and to make sure that you can accurately state the percentage of your home used for your business.

Step 1	Figure the total living area of your home in square footage; you may want to consult a property tax bill or real estate listing, as a starting point.
Step 2	Figure the area used regularly and exclusively for your business, including storage of inventory. Don't understate this number, but don't exaggerate it, either!
Step 3	Calculate the percentage of your home used for business (Step 2 divided by Step 1).

Step 4	Total up the following expenses for your home and multiply the total by the percentage from Step 3. In most cases, you will be able to deduct this percentage of these expenses:
	    * Casualty losses
	    * Deductible mortgage interest
	    * Real estate taxes

Step 5	Total up these additional expenses for your home and multiply the total by the percentage from Step 3. How much of these expenses you may deduct will be determined by a formula involving the "tentative profit" shown on line 29 of Schedule C.
	    * Excess mortgage interest
	    * Insurance
	    * Repairs and maintenance
	    * Utilities
	    * Other expenses
	    * Depreciation of your home

You may be allowed to carry over unallowed current-year expense deductions to a later year.

and the recipient organization's name, and take them with you whenever you drop off book donations at the library or anywhere else that qualifies you for a charitable contribution deduction. And you will be in even better shape if you have records to substantiate the amount that you paid for the donated books in the first place. Don't try to get away with claims of inflated values for those mass market paperback Len Deighton novels you've donated because you didn't want to sell them for a penny apiece; if you paid 25 cents each for them, that is the amount you can deduct. Appraisals and fair market values are irrelevant when you are a business owner and you acquired the material at a specific cost, and the IRS has shown an increasing interest of late in inflated donation values.

- As we've noted above, your "road trips" to acquire books, inspect bookstore inventories, and examine estate holdings are likely to generate considerable deductible expenses during the course of a tax year, regardless of whether they are day trips to the nearest college town or fortnights in Faulkner country. But these legitimate deductions will only hold up if you keep records showing their business purpose, cost, time, location, and who the other parties were.

- Be ready to substantiate all income and expenditures with receipts that match up with your bank deposits and expenses that are fully documented. If any of your business involves cash income or expenses, maintain complete records. And be sure to maintain business bank accounts that are completely separate from your personal accounts.

- File your tax return on time, and if you can't file it on time be sure to file the proper paperwork for an extension. Failing to file on time or get an authorized extension increases your chance of being noticed by the IRS, and while that's not always a bad thing, it is certainly never a good thing.

- In your zeal to claim legitimate deductions, beware of deducting so much that your household cannot possibly have survived on the remaining income. In many instances, your income level may trigger an audit. While the overall audit rate has gone down from 1989 to 1999, the IRS has been mandated to audit low-income items, most especially the earned income credit, according to a senior tax research analyst from H&R Block. So taxpayers with income that's less than $25,000 have seen an increase in audit rates over the years while the folks in the $100,000-plus cohort have seen their audit frequency drop.

Table 5: Projecting a Business Plan

Here are three models intended to illustrate how different levels of activity can produce different levels of results. As you see, we believe that the single most important benchmark in determining a month's sales is the number and price of desirable new listings a seller has posted at competitive prices in the past 30 days.

		Nice Part-Time Income	A Living Wage	A Successful Professional
1	Number of Books Listed	1,500	4,000	7,500
2	Number of New Listings Per Month	150	450	900
3	Average Gross Selling Price Per Book	$7.50	$8.00	$9.00
4	Percentage of Old Listings Sold/Month	5.0%	6.0%	7.0%
5	Percentage of New Listings Sold/Month	25.0%	30.0%	35.0%
6	Number of Books Sold/Month	113	375	840
7	Gross Monthly Revenue	$844	$3,000	$7,560
8	**Annual Revenue**	**$10,125**	**$36,000**	**$90,720**
9	Less Transaction Fees of 15%	-$1,519	-$5,400	-$13,608
10	**Net Annual Sales**	**$8,606**	**$30,600**	**$77,112**
11	Average Cost Per Book Sold	$0.50	$0.50	$0.50
12	Annual Cost of Goods Sold	$675	$2,250	$5,040
13	**Gross Annual Profit**	**$7,931**	**$28,350**	**$72,072**
14	**Monthly operating expenses**			
15	Phone line including all taxes and fees	$19	$38	$38
16	Online ISP monthly charge	$12	$24	$24
17	Internet Postage account	$15	$15	$15
18	Amazon monthly Pro Merchant fee	$40	$40	$40
19	Office expenses	$5	$10	$20
20	Automobile expense	$10	$20	$30
21	Sales tax*	$4	$15	$38
22	Licenses and fees	$5	$5	$5
23	**Total monthly operating expenses**	**$110**	**$167**	**$210**
24	**Total annual operating expenses**	**$1,322**	**$2,004**	**$2,517**
25	**Net pre-tax income**	**$6,609**	**$26,346**	**$69,555**
26	Less cash flow to inventory**	-$225	-$450	-$360
27	**Net cash flow**	**$6,384**	**$25,896**	**$69,195**

* Sales tax is projected only on sales made in a seller's own state, which are roughly estimated at 10 per cent for these purposes. This projection is based on a sales tax of 5%; obviously a seller should check his local state tax rate and adjust accordingly.

**"Cash flow to inventory" reflects the cost of goods for the growth of inventory, or (Line 2 minus Line 6 x Line 11 x 12 months).

XIV   Plans, Possibilities, And Pipedreams

If you run your business well and focus on constantly growing and relentlessly marketing your inventory, I believe you will reach the point eventually where your success at attaining some of your initial goals will inspire you to begin hatching plans and pipedreams for an even more prosperous future.   If you are able to approach this process with a calm and careful mindfulness of what has made you successful up to this point, it can be a wonderful and exciting period. If your path up to this point has been blazed with an entrepreneurial spirit, you will probably find that this next phase is an absolute necessity, lest boredom set in.   In any case, if you get to this point, you are certainly well-qualified to be your own guide to the future, and it is also a certainty that you already know and understand the strengths that you have which have made you successful, and perhaps you even understand the weaknesses that you have been able to avoid or overcome so as to avoid failing in this business endeavor.

I, therefore, will gladly settle for an opportunity to take a step back and serve as your business consultant for this next, very intriguing phase of activity.   Like many consultants, I will avoid giving much in the way of specific advice and instead will focus on a very general strategic approach, lightly season with a handful of fairly general, if stern, warnings.

Be Careful What You Wish For

Let's start here by listing three fairly predictable, knee-jerk propositions that often occur to successful online used booksellers when they began to think about the possibilities for expansion:

* expand your business to include a brick-and-mortar used bookshop;

* expand your business and make it scaleable, to use the unfortunate and usually hollow buzzword of the 21st century mega-capitalist, by hiring employees to acquire, list, and ship your books; and

146

- expand your business by setting up wholesale accounts with publishers and distributors and beginning to list and sell a catalog of new books.

Now, I am not saying that you can't succeed at any of these propositions. Probably you can. I simply want to ask yourself two very basic questions before you dive into any of these ideas:

- First, given the fact that each of these propositions requires a significant ongoing expenditure of cash, are you truly prepared for the introduction of these new stresses on your business and on your life?

- Second, if you take on these stresses, commit yourself to the ongoing expenditures, and *succeed*, what will you really have *gained?*

Lest you think that I am throwing rhetorical questions into your path out of some perverse desire to obstruct you, let me assure you that I would not do that. I will try to get more concrete.

Let's start by backing up and taking a look at the business model presented in this book, a business model at which you have presumably been successful.

- You began a successful business with an initial capital expenditure of less than $500 and ongoing expenses that came easily out of ongoing revenues without cutting seriously into profits.

- You've made no expensive ongoing commitments to employees, landlords, publishers, or distributors, so that -- at least in this particular business venture -- you have never had to worry about laying people off, failing to make payroll, failing to pay employer trust fund taxes, failing to make rent or accounts payable payments on time, being sued, filing for bankruptcy, having to box up returns, fielding telephone calls from creditors, having your assets attached, etc. Maybe you catch my drift.

Well, there is no point in beating a dead horse. If you succeed at adding the kind of expansion propositions we have been discussing here, I submit to you that you will have succeeded at re-inventing your business by going from new economy to old economy and saddling yourself with the need to supervise and pay a staff of employees, the need to show up for work each day somewhere other than the garage, basement, or extra bedroom (you'll need a little starch in the bathrobe), and the need to organize an accounts payable department and divert a serious and regular flow of cash through it to other entities which do not participate in buying your family's groceries or making the payments on your Lexus sport ute.

All the while, you will find that the quick-on-your-feet, fast-eat-the-slow capacity to tune in to, anticipate, and adapt to market changes will be lost or serious undercut by these new drains on your time, imagination, intellect, creativity, and energy. There are plenty of people reading this paragraph for whom imagination, intellect, creativity, and energy are the assets that give them competitive edge that makes them successful. But I believe those among you who will be most successful are those who are most mindful of these specific assets and who are most attentive to the need to protect their imagination, intellect, creativity, and energy from being overwhelmed by the drudgery and doom that might well result from the expansion ideas we have been discussing.

Okay. Enough of that. So, then, what kinds of ideas make good sense as ways to keep those entrepreneurial fires burning and to expand your business?

To begin with, it never hurts to look for new products, new markets, new customers, and new revenue that builds upon the things you already do and do well, or anticipates the products, markets, and customers that are right around the corner.

• *Affiliate fees*. If you have developed a website or if you regularly send out email to your customers, you may be able to build upon product suggestions or search links to Amazon or other e-commerce sites that will enable you to harvest affiliate-fee revenue through programs such as Amazon Associates or the kind of multi-affiliate program offered at Be Free (www.befree.com). Naturally a primary consideration with this kind of approach is the need to avoid "spamming" your customers with unsolicited commercial email.

Customers are glad to have a confirmation email from you, and probably won't mind an additional layer of book-related marketing information as long as it does not get in the way of the information they need to glean from the confirmation email, and as long as it includes a simple and user-friendly "remove" disclaimer at the end so that recipients will not be alarmed that your message is the first of one of those major, relentless spamming campaigns that we never seem to be able to turn off!

* ***Mine the potential for repeat customers.*** It is (or should be) understood that the vast majority of online buyers experience your business as an adjunct of Amazon.com or Alibris or Half.com or Advanced Book exchange, and will have "primary loyalty", if loyalty it is, to that larger entity. Nonetheless, as you operate your business over months and then years you are developing a valuable list of proven book buyers. Sending multiple commercial email messages to these customers is spam and you should not do it, but if sending one order confirmation gives you one or two free shots at these buyers, you may want to consider how you can most appropriately invite these folks to take advantage of special services you may provide such as free (or refunded) shipping on all repeat orders over $15, universal title search and fulfillment, a "build a library" service who are looking to collect a full set of Ludlum first editions or a representative library on a particular topic or even an incomplete set of two dozen or so Sweet Valley High page-turners. Along similar lines, we have found at Windwalker Books that roughly 5 per cent of all our sales are to "international customers," and these buyers seem especially responsive to our offers to help them avoid exorbitant global shipping costs by allowing them to come back with direct bulk orders.

* ***Sidelines.*** Sidelines involving music, software, videos, cards, artwork, magazines or magazine subscriptions, or other naturally complementary products often work well in brick-and-mortar stores, but each of these presents special problems for the online bookseller. While one can usually judge the condition of a used book in about ten seconds by eyeballing it inside and out, the same is not true for a used videocassette, DVD, CD, or CD-ROM.

- ***Anticipating Best Sellers.*** There's a certain category of books that can bring you regular sales and good profits, and all you have to do is see it coming and find the cheap copies while they are still cheap. At this writing, two of the best examples are Robert Ludlum's ***The Bourne Identity*** and Rebecca Wells' ***Divine Secrets of the Ya-Ya Sisterhood.*** In each case, they have been hyper-common in the past (to use the terminology of Chapter VI), with very good trade paperback editions selling online for well under a dollar each after having been phenomenally successful best sellers. They are, right now, the subject of films with very high-powered marketing campaigns in national print and television media, and they are flying off the shelves. If you had been aware six weeks ago that this would happen you could have purchased dozens of copies of each very cheaply, and you would be able to sell them very easily now for six to ten dollars each. The trick, obviously, is to anticipate these trends by availing yourself of the same information that is available – through the publishing and distribution industries -- to book buyers for new bookstores. You should be able to source this information yourself by conducting an online search of marketing information available from the major publishers such as Random House (with its ***atRandom*** newsletter), the large distributors such as Baker & Taylor, Koen Books, and Ingram, and trade publications such as ***Publisher's Weekly*** (which is very expensive, but carried by most public libraries). Frequently you will also find that, even after the demand for such a title has ramped up significantly and prices on Amazon's marketplace have risen accordingly, there are still plenty of inexpensive copies available at Half.com.

If you do decide to try out a new venture or idea, you may want to consider making it into a kind of "pilot project" at first with a different screen name or storefront so that the valuable online presence and reputation you have established with years of hard work is not trashed and tarnished overnight by unforeseen negative consequences of a new project.

Polish the Pearl

If the kinds of "new ideas" presented here have not really rung your bell, yet you also have not come up with anything you liked better, then perhaps we have accomplished our real purpose here in a backward kind of way. What I am getting at is the sense that our real mission ought to be simply to keep getting better and better as online booksellers. Polish the pearl, as oysters are wont to exhort one another down in the murky land of Spongebob Squarepants. I would hazard a guess that there are good ideas in this book that you have yet to try, and that will be even more true when the next edition comes along in a couple years or perhaps sooner. Try them. Hatch your own ideas, and try them. Get better. Be the best bookseller you can be.

Then, if you are indeed truly bored, maybe it is time to see if you can sell your business or pass it on to a friend or relative, and start something new. Try your hand at writing a book on the subject. Is this just a tongue-in-cheek suggestion? Not entirely. There is certainly room for more than one book on the subject, and I would rather see them be written by people who have walked the walk rather than those whose only skill involves talking the talk. If you don't have the desire to write such a book yourself, but you do have some ideas about how this one could be made better, I hope you will take the step of sending me an email at Windwalker@nativeweb.net. I promise that I will read it and try to use your thoughts to help make the next edition better so that the noble profession of bookselling, about which I rhapsodized much earlier in this book, will be even better served by the nouveau profession of online bookselling. Thank you. You are free to go and sell books. And I am free to return to my own first love, books and bookselling, for which my passion only grows stronger.

APPENDICES

Appendix 1: Glossary

The beginning point for the following glossary was a very fine "Book Collector's Glossary" compiled by Carl Noe and viewable both at rec.collecting.books, where it was first posted August 23, 1996, and at www.trussel.com/books/glossary.htm. "It is not complete, but is a work in progress, and a labor of love for those who collect books," writes Carl. "It is dedicated to Scot Kamins (rec.collecting.books proponent) who edited it for me." We salute Carl for a fine piece of work and thank him for allowing us to use it here. (**Starred * items** are our additions).

academic reprints Items published by a photographic process for the academic market when a scholarly work, for which there is relatively little demand after its original edition, requires a new printing.

addendum, *pl.* **addenda** A supplement to a book. When material needs to be added to a finished book at the time of its binding, it may be printed on a slip of paper and tipped in, or pasted in.

advance copy A review copy. When a book is published, complimentary advance copies will often be sent to reviewers.

advance reading copy * Another name for an advance copy, whose sale is prohibited on Amazon

Americana A classification of books and other objects having to do with America, its people and their history (generally considered to bear relation to the United States of America by those residing in North America).

annotated Including critical and explanatory notes.

antiquarian Of old, rare books, or one who deals in them.

apocryphal A work which is of doubtful authenticity or authorship.

appendix The additional or supplementary material sometimes found at the end of a book.

association copy * A copy that previously belonged to the author, which has been signed or annotated or inscribed with a gift inscription by the author, or someone linked to the author of book in some way, or, sometimes, some other interesting personality

atlas folio Description of the size of a book: about 25 inches high.

author's copies Complimentary copies of the first edition of a book given to the author by the publisher.

autograph The author's signature, typically found on the title page or flyleaf of a book.

backbone A book's backstrap, backstrip or spine.

bar code The common term for Universal Product Code.

bds. Abbreviation for "boards," which see.

belles lettres Fine arts literature (fiction, poetry, drama, etc.) as distinguished from scientific/technical writing.

Biblio An electronic mailing list which is dedicated to news of the used book trade.

bibliography * A list of works on a given subject or by a given author

bibliomane A book-nut (or worse ;).

bibliophile A book lover (or worse ;).

blurb The paragraph or so printed on the cover or dust jacket of a book which almost always tells you how important the book is.

boards The stiff front and back parts of a hardcover book.

bound galley An uncorrected page or galley proof sent out by a publisher before publication for publicity.

bowdlerization The practice of censorship by publication of expurgated texts. This practice got its name from English editor Thomas Bowdler (1854-1825) who published altered editions (especially of Shakespeare's works).

casebound A hardcover book.

chapbook A small, usually paperback, book of poetry or a religious tract or somesuch.

chipped A condition in which small pieces of the dust jacket have been chipped away at the edges

clothbound A book with cloth covering the boards.

codex A volume of ancient manuscript.

colophon Either a publisher's trademark or information concerning the book's publication printed at the end of a book. Literally the finishing stroke.

comb binding A binding similar to a spiral binding, but made of plastic, and which if flattened would resemble a comb.

deaccessioning Selling or otherwise disposing of books from a collection.

deckle edge Rough edges which a sheet of paper has after it has left the deckle, but before it is trimmed in the papermaking process.

definitive edition The most authoritative version of a work.

desideratum, *pl.* **desiderata** Something needed and wanted. Desiderata is a want list.

dust jacket The paper cover (d.j.).

dust wrapper The same as a dust jacket (d.w.).

double elephant folio Description of the size of a book: about 50 inches high.

duodecimo Description of the size of a book: about 7.75 inches high (12mo).

edition All the copies of the book made from a specific set of type (with the exception of minor alterations).

elephant folio Description of the size of a book: about 23 inches high.

embossing A process which produces decorations raised above the surface (typically of printable material).

endpaper The folded sheet of paper pasted to the inside of the front or back cover and attached to the edge of the first or last page of a hardcover book during manufacturing. Endpapers are not normally numbered.

erratum, *pl.* **errata** A correction of error(s) inserted into a book after it has been printed.

ex library A book with library markings on it.

ex libris A Latin phrase meaning, "From the Library of."

even folio Page numbers on the left-hand pages.

FS For sale.

facsimile edition An exact reproduction of an original book depicting the text and the book's physical appearance.

fair condition A worn book with defects such as a torn dust jacket, foxing, or loose binding, etc.

fine condition Nearly new, with slight signs of aging, but no defects.

first edition The first printing of the first edition (as far as collectors are concerned).

flyleaf Unprinted pages (other than endpapers) which may appear at the front or back of a book.

folio Description of the size of a book: about 15 inches high (Fo).

fore edge The front of a book, considering the spine to be the back of a book.

fore-edge painting A form of book decoration popular in the late eighteenth century which displays a painting when the books pages are fanned.

fortyeightmo Description of the size of a book: about 4 inches high (48mo).

foxed Discolored, usually with reddish-brown spots, especially the leaves of a book.

frontispiece Illustration which faces the title page.

galley A proof of a book made before the pages are numbered.

gauffering (goffering) Decorative, deckle edged pages.

good condition A complete book with no major defects, showing normal wear and ageing.

gutter White space between facing pages.

headband A decorative cloth band added to the top of bottom of a book's spine.

holograph A document handwritten by the person purported to have written it.

hornbook A child's primer, made of parchment, mounted on a board with a handle, protected by a transparent plate made of horn.

i.p. In print.

illuminated Old manuscripts and early books decorated with ornamental letters or colored illustrations.

illustrated Decorated with pictures or other features usually for the purpose of clarifying the context.

impression The number of books printed in a press run, or the run itself.

imprint The publisher's and/or printer's note usually found at the foot of the title page giving place, date and publication information.

incunabulum, *pl.* **incunabula** A book from the "cradle" time of printing (before 1500).

library binding A reinforced binding.

limited edition A printing which is limited to a stated number. Often inscribed with the author's signature and a sequence number.

mint condition Term referring to a used or antiquarian book whose condition is "Like new". This term is more proper to numismatics and philately, with antiquarians usually preferring "as new."

nom de plume Literally "pen name," the pseudonym an author uses.

o.p. Out of print.

octavo Description of the size of a book: about 9.75 inches high (8mo).

parchment Animal skin (usually sheep) used for a writing material.

quarto Description of the size of a book: about 12 inches high (4mo).

reading copy A book which has little or no value as a collectible item, but has complete text.

recto The right-hand or front of a book leaf. Contrast "verso," the back of the leaf.

shaken A condition characterized by very loose binding.

sixteenmo Description of the size of a book: about 6.75 inches high (16mo).

sixtyfourmo Description of the size of a book: about 3 inches high (64mo).

stacked A condition characterized by a shift in the binding of a book.

thirtytwomo Description of the size of a book: about 5 inches high (32mo).

tooling Decoration of a book's cover by impression of gold leaf or other material.

twentyfourmo Description of the size of a book: about 5.75 inches high (24mo).

vanity publisher One who publishes a book paid for by the author.

vellum A fine calfskin used for writing or book manufacture (used for most ancient manuscripts).

verso The back of a leaf. Contrast "verso," the front of the leaf.

very good condition A complete book, as issued, with very few blemishes or signs of wear.

WTB Want to buy.

WTT Want to trade.

widow A single word or partial line.

woodcut A block of wood which is engraved for printing or the resulting product of its use.

zinc etching A photoengraving process which produces black-and-white line drawings.

Appendix 2: Standard Bookseller Abbreviations

We suggest that you use considerable discretion in determining which abbreviations to employ in describing your books for online sales. If you are listing a book about book collecting, don't be shy with the terminology and the abbreviations. If you are listing a copy of **Sounder** or **Seeds of Yesterday**, even an abbreviation like "VG" or "mass mkt pbk" may be too obscure. It's always nice to be concise, but if your brevity comes at the cost of clarity the potential buyer is likely to move on to the next available copy of a title.

One good rule of thumb that is probably so obvious I should be embarrassed to state it is simply that you should only use an abbreviation when you are relatively confident that the potential buyer is likely to be familiar with, and understand, the word or words for which the abbreviation stands. There, I've stated it, and I am not embarrassed.

ABA ......American Bookseller's Association. Also: Antiquarian Booksellers' Association (the British equivalent of the ABAA)

ABAA ..... Antiquarian Booksellers' Association of America.

A.E.G......All Edges Gilt.

ALS .... Autographed Letter Signed.

ARC......Advance Reading Copy

BCE......Book Club Edition.

BDS......Boards

BOMC......Book-of-the-Month Club.

C........ Small c before date meaning circa; around/about referring to date

CP or ©....... Copyright.

CWO......Check or cash with order.

DEC....... Decorated.

DJ......Dust jacket.

DS...... Document signed.

DW........Dustwrapper (same as dust jacket, or book jacket)

ED.......Edition or Editor.

EP........Endpaper

EX. LIB......Ex. Library copy.

EX. LIBRIS...From the library of, referring to previous owner. Often found on bookplates.

F.........Fine

FFEP......Front free endpaper.

FL........ . .Flyleaf.

FRONTIS... ....Frontispiece.

G........ ..Good.

HC........Hardcover

IL. ILLUS.....Illustrated.

IOBA...... ...Independent Online Booksellers Association.

LITHO........Lithograph.

LTD. ED........Limited Edition.

N.D (or n-d)........No Date.

N.P (or n-pl)........No Place

O or OOP..........Out-of-Print.

PP...... ...Pages. p. (and then the number) for page ../pp. For pages - to--

PPB.......Paperback

PPD.......Postpaid.

PR.........Printing

PSEUD. ......Pseudonym.

PUB.......Published/publisher.

RFEP.......Rear free endpaper.

RET.........Returnable.

SLC..........Slipcase

SGD.......Signed.

SP........Spelling.

T.E.G. ....Top Edge Gilt.

TLS.........Typed letter signed.

TP........Title Page.

VG........Very Good.

VOL., VOLS.....Volume/Volumes.

W.A.F.......With All Faults.

W/O.......Without.

Appendix 3: A Casual Bibliography

My friend and colleague Genevieve Kazdin is the proprietor of a very well-run online bookshop on Cape Cod, called Dunes Studio, and she has distilled years of experience and education into the following casual, annotated bibliography of books about bookselling and book collecting. I thank her heartily for her contribution, her good humor, and her support, and I urge everyone who finds this bibliography helpful or illuminating or amusing, or not, to go directly to her online storefront at www.amazon.com/shops/dunesstudio and buy one or two of her listings, which I can assure you from personal experience will then arrive promptly in very careful packaging.

Books

Collected Books: The Guide To Values 2002. Allen Ahearn, Patricia Ahearn. 2002, Putnam, 0399147810.

Expensive, but an excellent guide to relative values. Beware - the market changes quickly and such a book can be outdated before it hits the stores. It does help in setting values, however.

Book of First Books. Allen Ahearn. 1983, 0961049413.

Do you remember Larry McMurtry's first book? It can be important to know the titles of the first books of current popular authors. Ahearn is a great help in tracking down this information.

Price Guide to Cookbooks and Recipe Leaflets (1991 values). Linda J. Dickinson. Collector Books, Schroeder Publishing Co., Inc.

Some interesting and little-known titles. Remember, values quickly go out of date, but this book can help assign publication dates to books and leaflets with little information.

Huxford's Old Book Value Guide. 1999, Collector Books, Schroeder Publishing Co. Inc. 11th edition, 1574321196.

Again, such guides quickly go out of date and should not be used as absolute pricing guidelines. The value of this book, for me, is giving publication dates and information for many books, and clues as to their relative values to the author's other works.

Used and Rare: Travels in the Book World. Lawrence and Nancy Goldstone. 1997 Thomas Dunne Book, St. Martin's Press 0312187688.

A charming, chatty memoir of the book collection adventures of a likeable couple finding their way from small, friendly used book stores to the highest level of collecting experiences. The reader learns along with the Goldstones.

A Gentle Madness. Nicholas A. Basbanes. 1999 Owl Book, Henry Holt 0805061762.

Passionate about books? Read about some of the great, renowned collectors, many with unlimited funds, and some with minimal assets. This is essential reading for anyone seriously collecting, or even dreaming about it.

Cyber Rules: Strategies for Excelling at E-Business. Thomas M. Siebel and Pat House. 1999 Currency Book, Doubleday 0385494122.

An interesting view of e-business which offers thoughts and suggestions for success even for the small business person. Anyone who takes online selling seriously should take a look at the large picture of e-business.

Booked To Die. John Dunning. PocketBooks, 2000, 0743410653.

The Bookman's Wake. John Dunning. PocketBooks 1995 0671567829.

What are two mystery novels doing in this list? Dunning's character, Cliff Janeway, is an ex-homicide detective who has turned in his badge and opened a book store. The mysteries revolve around rare books, the finding of them, book scouts, and other attributes of the book business. Dunning seems to have researched this well, and therefore this is a pleasant way to pick up some of the tricks of the trade.

Parnassus on Wheels. Christopher Morley. Common Reader Edition, Trafalgar Sq., 2000 , 1888173564.

Haunted Bookshop. Christopher Morley. Common Reader Edition, Trafalgar Sq., 2000, 1888173572.

And now for something completely different. These small tales are somewhere between romance and adventure. They were written about 1917, and are as old fashioned as you might guess. When Roger Mifflin meets up with Helen McGill, they elope together in Roger's wagon and travel around selling books. Eventually, they settle in Brooklyn and open a store. Maybe they will not help you sell books, but they will put a smile on your face, and share the book-magic that Roger and Helen felt. Not bad, for a summer day's read!

Book Finds. Ian C. Ellis. 2001, Perigee Books, Berkley Publishing 0399526544.

I find this an enormously helpful book. There, I said it. Other online dealers have scoffed at this one, but I find it contains a great deal of information: a glossary; help in identifying first editions, BCEs; reference suggestions; and perhaps most helpful of all, the attitude that book selling can be done well and with ethics intact. Ellis wisely does not publish a price guide for books he recommends. He knows how misleading such a guide can be after only a short time. This book is worth reading -- and if you do not find it of value, why, resell it online!

Slightly Chipped: Footnotes in Booklore. Lawrence and Nancy Goldstone, 0312205872, May 1999, Thomas Dunne Books, St. Martin's Press.

The further book-collecting adventures of the Goldstones, as easy-to-read, and informative as their earlier book. One learns with this couple and has a good read as well. The value of catalogues, why the touch and feel of a book can be important, and the atmosphere of a book sale are just some of the aspects covered here.

BOOKS: Identification and price guide (The Confident Collector). Nancy Wright, 0380769417, September 1993, Avon Books trade paper.

A discussion and listing of collectible books, with obviously out-dated values, presenting sane arguments on the policies of pricing used books for sale.

Cookbooks Worth Collecting. Mary Barile, 0870696866, 1994, Wallace-Homestead, Chilton Books, Radnor Pennsylvania.

A treasure of information about collectible cookbooks, with history, descriptions, photos, and suggested prices. An excellent resource for specialists.

Unsigned: A Booklover's Mystery by Julie Wallin Kaewert (Mass Market Paperback - January 2001) Bantam Books ISBN: 0553582194.

Unsolicited: A Booklover's Mystery by Julie Wallin Kaewert (Mass Market Paperback - August 2000) Crime Line ISBN: 0553582097.

Unbound: A Booklover's Mystery by Julie Wallin Kaewert (Mass Market Paperback - December 1997) Bantam Books ISBN: 0553577158.

Untitled: A Booklover's Mystery by Julie Wallin Kaewert (Mass Market Paperback) Bantam Books ISBN: 0553577174.

Uncatalogued by Julie Wallin Kaewert (Mass Market Paperback - January 2002) Crime Line ISBN: 0553582208.

Another delicious series of mysteries set in a British publishing house. If we are reading for pleasure and relaxation, we might as well pick up the terms used in the publishing business and come away with a sense of the industry. Who says earning needs to be boring?

The Elements of Style. William Strunk, Jr and E. B. White.

It is my sincere belief that an effective book seller must not only know books, but be articulate and precise in language. Since many have difficulties with spelling (use a good spell-checker) and with the vagaries of English grammar, I recommend this small, concise volume as perhaps the easiest way to refresh all those rules we learned in third grade. I, personally, tend not to buy from someone who can't cope with the differences among there, their, and they're.

Periodicals

Firsts, the Book Collector's Magazine is published 10 times a year (monthly except for July and August.). Subscriptions are $40 to the US, $60 US to Canada, $95 US to all other countries. (www.firsts.com). Kathryn Smiley, Editor, Tucson, AZ.

Each issue features various articles on one subject. (December 2001 concentrated on American Gift Books.) One also finds news of catalogues, sales, classified ads. This magazine is essential for anyone specializing in first editions.

Book: The Magazine for the Reading Life (www.bookmagazine.com). Subscriptions are $20 for six bimonthly issues. Jerome V. Kramer, Editor; West Egg Communications, New York, NY.

Book presents news and reviews about current releases, upcoming releases, interviews with authors, and a wide range of reviews.

Pages: The Magazine for People Who Love Books (www.ireadpages.com). Subscriptions are $15.95 for six bimonthly issues. John Hogan, Editor-In-Chief, San Diego CA.

On the surface, this magazine is similar to ***Book***. Together, they encompass a broad look at current publications, and offer a variety of reviewers with differing viewpoints. A valuable pair of periodicals for anyone wanting to be aware of what's new in the book world.

Appendix 4: An Online Bookseller's Rolodex

What follows is a rude beginning, compiling links to sites that are mentioned throughout this book. We've left plenty of white space for you to add your own notes, phone numbers, editions, personal contact names, and to-do lists, on the off chance you are not planning to re-sell this book.

Book Search Engines

www.Bookfinder.com

Addall used.addall.com and www.addall.com

Inventory Management Software

Booktrakker (www.booktrakker.com)

BookHound (www.bookhound.net)

BookRouter (www.bookrouter.com)

Price Hunter (www.saveallsoft.com)

Bookseller Organizations

American Booksellers Association
(www.bookweb.org, email: info@bookweb.org)

Independent Online Booksellers Association
(www.ioba.org)

International Book Collectors Association
(www.rarebooks.org)

Antiquarian Booksellers' Association of America
(www.abaa.org)

Bookseller Mailing Lists and Message Boards

Bibliophile Mailing List(www.bibliophilegroup.com)

Amazon.com Seller Connection Discussion Board

(http://forums.prosperotechnologies.com/am-sellconnect/start/)

Book Distributors

Daedalus Books (www.daedalus-books.com)

Links with Information of Interest to Booksellers

Book Sale Finder (www.booksalefinder.com)

Glenn Larson's Guide to First Edition Identification on the International Book Collector's Association website at www.rarebooks.org/firsted.htm

Bibliomania on Grading Definitions (www.bibliomania.net/Lesson1.html)

Independent Online Booksellers Association on Book Descriptions (www.ioba.org/desc.html)

Internal Revenue Service (www.irs.gov)

Amazon Associates – Affiliate Referrals (www.amazon.com/associates)

Be Free – Multi-Affiliate Programs (www.befree.com).

AuctionBytes (www.auctionbytes.com)

www.bookhunterpress.com

PublishersWeekly.com

www.nytimes.com

www.Gomez.com

The Midlist Study Group Report: A committee appointed by the Authors Guild set out a year ago to study the problem of the "midlist" book. With the help of a grant from George Soros's Open Society Institute, the committee hired the reporter David D. Kirkpatrick to research and write about what he found. Kirkpatrick is the ***Times*** reporter who wrote the news story on used book sales quoted in Chapter II of this book. www.authorsguild.org/prmidlist.html

Shipping Carriers

United States Postal Service (www.usps.com)

United Parcel Service (www.ups.com)

Federal Express (www.fedex.com)

Buying Postage Online

www.endicia.com

www.stamps.com

Neopost's Simply Postage (www.neopost.com)

Pitney Bowes' Clickstamp (www.pitneyworks.com).

Shipping Supplies and Solutions

www.associatedbag.com

www.transparentmail.com

ULINE Shipping Supplies (www.uline.com)

Hillas Packaging Network (www.hillas.com)

Papermart (www.papermart.com)

Book Repairs

Book Repair, by Elizabeth Dodds, Colby College Libraries (www.colby.edu/library/collections/technical_services/wp/BookRepair.html)

A Simple Book Repair Manual, Preservation Services, Dartmouth College Library (http://www.dartmouth.edu/~preserve/repair/repairindex.htm)

Emergency Salvage of Moldy Books and Paper, by Beth Lindblom Patkus, Northeast Document Conservation Center (http://www.nedcc.org/plam3/tleaf39.htm)

Book Deodorizing granules from J Godsey Booksellers (email: gods@attbi.com)

Online Banking, Payment & Merchant Accounts

Netbank (www.netbank.com)

First Internet Bank of Indiana (www.firstib.com)

PayPal (www.paypal.com)

ProPay (www.propay.com)

Quickbooks Merchant Account Service (www.quickbooks.com/services/mas/more.html)

Email
Nativeweb (www.nativeweb.net)

Booksellers Venues

Amazon Marketplace:
URL: www.amazon.com/marketplace
EMAIL: sellers-support@amazon.com
TELEPHONE: 800-201-7575 or 877-251-0696 (Between 6 a.m. and 7 p.m. Pacific time, Monday through Friday)
FAX: 206-266-2950

Amazon zShops and Auctions
URL: www.amazon.com/zshops
EMAIL: seller-support@amazon.com; community-help@amazon.com - report a community rules violation; reports@amazon.com - report abuse
TELEPHONE: 800-201-7575 or 877-251-0696 (Between 6 a.m. and 7 p.m. Pacific time, Monday through Friday)
FAX: 206-266-2950

Half.com
URL: www.half.ebay.com/products/books/index.cfm
EMAIL: books@half.com or Info@half.com
TELEPHONE: (888) 879-4253 or 1 (800) 545-9857

EBay Auctions
URL: www.ebay.com
EMAIL: eBay discourages direct email contact by does provide a web-based email support system at www.pages.ebay.com/help/basics/select-support.html

Advanced Book Exchange
URL: www.abebooks.com
EMAIL: ABE Financial: invoice@abebooks.com; ABE/Half.com Program: half.com@abebooks.com; Web-based "Help Wizard" at www.dogbert.abebooks.com/abe/ActionRequestInsert
TELEPHONE: 1-800-315-5335 6AM-10PM Mon-Fri; 10AM-2PM Sat PST
FAX: 1 - 250 - 475 - 6016

Alibris
URL: www.alibris.com
EMAIL: sellers@alibris.com
SNAIL MAIL: Alibris, 1250 45th Street, Suite 100 Emeryville, CA 94608.

Antiqbook
URL: www.antiqbook.com
EMAIL: nan@antiqbook.nl

BiblioDirect.com
URL: www.BiblioDirect.com
EMAIL: admin@BiblioDirect.com .

Bibliology
URL: www.bibliology.com
EMAIL:membership@bibliology.com or enquries@bibliology.com

Biblion
URL: www.biblion.com
EMAIL: www.biblion.com/contact.php
TELEPHONE: 020 7495 0219, between 9am and 6pm GMT Monday to Friday.

Bibliophile
URL: www.bibliophile.net
EMAIL: benson@bibliophile.net
TELEPHONE: +41 1 364 57 11

BookAvenue
URL: www.bookavenue.co
EMAIL: info@bookavenue.com

Books & Collectibles
URL: www.booksandcollectibles.com.au
EMAIL: admin@booksandcollectibles.com.au

TomFolio
URL: www.tomfolio.com
EMAIL: www.tomfolio.com/sendmessage.asp?type=2
SNAIL MAIL: TomFolio, P.O. Box 392, Readville, MA 02137